Lisa J. Marshall

First published in 2020
By Dennison Press
PO Box 221
Aaronsburg, PA 16820
USA

A catalog record for this book
is available from the Library of Congress.

ISBN 978-1-7362370-0-7

Printed in the United States of America

1st Printing 2020

Table of Contents

To My Readers

ommon wisdom is that one writes with an audience in mind. Unfortunately, that has never worked for me. I write because something has seized me by the scruff of the neck and won't let go. It wants to be said, and is using me to say it. Only later can I figure out who is supposed to hear/read it.

So it was with ***Yin***. Fortuitously, my daughters were NOT having it. 'Who's this for, Mom?" they kept asking. And at some point, I realized it was, more than anything, for *them:* Millennial women (and men). And for those coming after. For those young people who were told there was no bias when there was. For those for whom full equality and opportunity were promised but not delivered. Those who were promised a level playing field economically, only to find it was a sham, a charade. Those who were discovering that "being one of the guys" was a shallow victory that cost far too much--cost, in fact, their voice.

And for all of us, female and male. All who struggle to find their full, rich, resonant voice, to sing the song only they can sing, make the art only they can make, lead the organizations only they can lead, plant the garden only they can plant. Because voices take many forms. And, as with the blues, only when we've faced the darkness can we really offer the light and sing the song fully.

Why aren't there more stories in here? "Stories would show us how it could be done," one colleague said. Because **you already**

know the most important stories, dear reader. They're the ones you've experienced and hidden, haven't told, been afraid to recognize and honor. You know how your voice has been silenced, how Yang enhanced your fear of Yin, kept you afraid of the dark--the composting, the rotting, the turning of your ego into the humus in which something new and magnificent could grow. So rather than feeding you others' stories, I'm suggesting that you pay attention to ***your*** story.

My hope is that ***Yin*** will give you the courage, the confidence and the strength to own it, tell it and, where needed, change it. To help you do that, ***Yin*** is designed to be a conversation with yourself, about yourself. I've put a set of questions, and left room for you to make notes at the end of every chapter, notes that will help you excavate, explore and reshape your story to one in which you can be and are your fullest, most wondrous self.

So this is a book to think on and write in, as you explore your own journey to leadership maturity. It is not a book to inhale, so much as sip. Read a chapter, think about it, journal about the questions and reflect some more before you head off to the next chapter. Allow time and space, and give yourself the gift of deep absorption. A voice is a terrible thing to waste.

Prologue

Sixteen years ago I published a book, ***Speak the Truth and Point to Hope; The Leader's Journey to Maturity***, on what I'd learned about leadership and maturity from my leadership coaching practice. I wanted to stake a claim for the primary role of love in leading. I used Joseph Campbell's *The Hero's Journey* and the concept of archetypes to structure the book. Since then, I've been asked many times "but does that concept apply to women?" My answer has always been, "Yes! If you're not the hero in your own story, who is?" And still........there *was* something missing, something different.

Many years later, Hyemeyohsts Storm, friend and mentor, author of ***Seven Arrows*** and other books on the cosmology of America's First Nations, read ***Speak the Truth*** and told me, "This is a good book, Lisa, but you have to write a book on leadership for women."

I was flummoxed: I had worked hard to make sure ***Speak the Truth*** was a book about leadership for *everyone*. And looking back at it now, in many ways I did. I tried rewriting it and failed: I didn't really seem to have anything new to say. I still believe what I said then: love is ultimately the key to effective leadership. So how *is* the journey to maturity different for women? As these things often do, it took a long time, and then a very specific convergence of experiences for the answer to become a blinding flash of the obvious.

#MeToo. Woman after woman stood up to tell her story. Stories that had been told and silenced, stories that had never been told, out of a fear of losing life or livelihood, or being seen as weak, incapable of holding one's own. Hearing these stories, day after day, I suddenly saw what had been in front of me all along: The Journey IS different (and it is the same.) The difference is that women (mostly) don't go after the Golden Fleece or Medusa's head. What I now call the Yin journey (or pilgrimage) is interior: we go inside to find our voice.

And in finding our voice, we frequently "give voice" to a deeper collective unconscious, what author and consultant Meg Wheatley calls "what wants and needs to happen." We ask different questions. We make what is felt implicitly explicit and whole. Experiencing this vast wave of women finally saying "It happened, it wasn't ok. And it still isn't," I could finally grasp how the Yin version of the Hero's Journey was different.

While the Yang version of the Journey story is about external striving, learning and growth from being organized and focused, about grasping the Golden Fleece and winning the battles, the Yin journey is internal, to find one's voice and bring *that* gift--its insight, concerns, caring and wisdom--into the world. It is in service of giving voice and presence to that which is felt, yet is unspoken and unseen. For both Yin and Yang, the goal is always ultimately to bring something of great value to one's community.

A lot has happened in a couple decades. As I began to explore what new needed to be said--for women *and* men--about the leadership journey, I realized that an exploration of Yin was central to that journey. I also discovered the juicy new thinking that has emerged around the concept of development in our physical, spiritual, emotional and intellectual domains. Our understanding of maturity has been vastly enriched. Thus began a new journey.......

Chapter One: Where Do We Start?

e start, as I am writing this, from the year 2020. We start from lockdown in the time of Covid. We start from the reality of pandemic, of a deadly and little understood killer disease that is clearly the result of our globalized, interlocked, inter-webbed, interwoven world. And we start from Black Lives Matter and #MeToo, a time of protest, a time when injustice lies exposed and bleeding.

We start from a world inflamed and often aflame. We start from a planet under siege by its inhabitants. We start from a world driven by a cancerous concept of growth at all costs, damn the consequences. We start from a place where the curtain has been pulled back on the flimsy structures that were the underpinnings of our "global economy," and the terrible injustices propping it up stand clearly revealed.

We start from a concept of "civilization" that requires vast disconnection--from the planet, from our ancestors, from our communities and from ourselves. We start from loneliness, depression, isolation and despair.

We start from a world whose carrying capacity has been exceeded.[1] We start from a world that still believes there is an "away", a place to get rid of the junk we have accumulated in an attempt to fill the voids in lives that have no sense of purpose.

We start from a world where identities as citizens have been replaced by identities as consumers.[2] We start from a normal that never should have been normalized.

We also start from a rare moment of possibility, when many things that people thought would never change have, in fact, quickly and dramatically changed. We start from a liminal doorway, where the old "normal" still pulls us and a new normal beckons but has yet to reveal itself. We start from a moment of choice.

One choice is to return as closely as we can to the old "normal." To the dysfunctional relationships we have with the planet and with one another--our governments, our legal systems, our educational systems, our economic systems. Systems thinker Gregory Bateson long ago observed, "*That is the paradigm: Treat the symptom to make the world safe for the pathology.*"[3] Our centuries-long experiment with unchecked growth "is self-terminating. Either we figure out a way to end it ourselves, or it does the job for us."[4]

Or we could build new stories. We could, as economist Kate Raworth, author of ***Doughnut Economics***, has written, opt for economies that make us thrive over economies that insist on growth. (The doughnut is the space in which thriving is possible.) She observes that it is "most striking...that many of the policies proposed for enabling an economy to be growth-agnostic[5] could help drive it towards being distributive and regenerative by design." We could, for example, develop a new story about the way businesses and governments work together, as economist Marianna Mazzucato proposes, such that governments--and the people they serve--benefit from the R&D they fund. [6]

We could, as biologist Janine Benyus proposes, choose to learn from nature rather than consume it. We could, as Donella Meadows, environmental scientist and author of ***Limits to Growth*** observed, recognize that "effective systems tend to have three properties--healthy hierarchy, self-organization and resilience --and so should be stewarded to enable these characteristics to emerge.[7] We could, as Courtney Martin proposes, redefine "better off" as having clean air, clean water, less "stuff" and less stress.

We could rebuild the concept of the commons and the common good, using the rules Nobel Prize winning economist Elinor Ostrom identified, rules we know work. We could heal trauma--ours and our ancestors'--and not pass it on to our children. We could learn to listen to the plants and the planet, learn to heal from the medicines plants provide us rather than ones industrially engineered.

We could acknowledge, as Rebeca Solnit has documented in ***A Paradise Built in Hell***, that self-organized communities get far more done with far greater efficiency in times of need. We could deliberately restrict governmental powers so that bureaucracies cannot destroy citizen efforts during crises. And we could create governments in which "public servants" understand what that phrase really means.

We could, as activist, attorney and author Valerie Kaur proposes, learn to love our enemies as ourselves–and learn to love ourselves. We could learn to balance rage with love, to listen in ways that make us see everyone's pain, and in doing so, reimagine the world into the "beloved community" for which we all yearn.[8]

We could create stories about leadership wherein maturity and stewardship are what matter, instead of our current Peter Pan story of playing the same games over and over and never growing up.

We could, as young climate change fighters Autumn Peltier (Canada), Mari Copeny (Flint, Mich.) Artemisa Xajruaba (Brazil) and Greta Thunberg (Sweden) have asked, step up to our responsibilities as adults for creating a world where the next generation of children **can** thrive, instead of a world being wrecked by the consequences of climate change.

We could create a world where the feminine values of caring, conserving and creating are spoken, valued and respected. Where white women are Allies, not Beckys, Karens or Amy Coopers, recognizing and drawing on their own experiences of being ignored and oppressed instead of defaulting to their ugly heritage of so-called racial superiority and learned helplessness.

A world where community and individuality are both honored. Where children are loved and elderhood is aspired to, a world in which no one is left behind. A world full of the gifts of the imagination--stories, poetry, art, theatre, and beauty. A world where Yin voices are heard and honored. A world where love reigns. A world where Yin and Yang are in balance.

---

[1] Term from the ecological sciences denoting the range a natural system can occupy before it either floods or dries up/starves
[2] I believe I first learned this phrase from Sister Joan Chittester, decades ago
[3] https://medium.com/future-crunch/portal-economics-ae11000a4f4d
[4] Ibid.
[5] As opposed to growth-driven
[6] Kate Raworth, ***Doughnut Economics***. p. 230
[7] Ibid, p. 136
[8] Kaur, Valarie, ***Seen No Stranger, Part I***

Your Story

1. From where does your story start?

2. What aspects of the old "normal" still call to you? What do you want to conserve/keep/preserve?

3. What are you ready to let go of?

4. What would you like to see become part of your new "normal"? What changes call to you?

Chapter Two: What Do I Mean by Yin?

In ancient Chinese Taoist thinking, Yin was the feminine principal, represented by the dark side of the Tao symbol. In Webster's definition, it stands for darkness, coldness and death[1], to which passivity is often added. In her two-volume series, ***Ancient Mirrors of Womanhood***, Merlin Stone notes that in the ***Tao Te Ching,*** Yin does not, in fact, imply passivity so much as receptivity, the ability to move with what *is*. Her example is the way water flows around the boulder, rather than the "more aggressive Yang" way of crashing over it. She describes Yin as "the female principle of following the strategy that, to some, might seem passive, yet in the long run, is most likely to assure a reaching of the destination."[2]

To me, Yin is neither primarily male nor female. It is, however, what is missing in the world today. It is also the dark, moist and fertile interior world, whether in ourselves or on the planet, from which all growth comes. Biologists now estimate that something like 80% of living biomass is below the earth's surface. The planet itself is profoundly Yin!

Like the oceans, or Ireland's ancient wells (protected by magical well-maidens in Celtic mythology), Yin is the life-giving, watery darkness from which we came and to which we ultimately return.

During our lifetimes, we need to visit that world, perhaps on more than one occasion, in order to compost our former life into fertile ground for a new one.[3] Yin represents un-seeable processes

--like seeds turning into plants, or the caterpillar's transformation into the butterfly. It holds the diffuse context in which women have historically operated, circling around something vague, until suddenly it takes luminous form without our appearing to have "done" something. And it requires a giving over to that process, no longer insisting that we humans are in charge, or should be given credit.

Some examples:

Healing is Yin. By that I mean two things: 1.) Yin is literally what the healing process is--an interior, mysterious, powerful force that requires darkness, sleep *and* rest, ceding control to forces bigger than oneself. Our bodies do not heal during our waking hours. To heal requires a descent into darkness, timelessness, facing deep pain in order to be remade, reborn as something new, on a timeline not of one's own choosing. Periods of relative ease, punctuated by sharp pains, intense burning, unexplained prickles, dull aches, intense itching, are part of the process, be it physical or emotional. The reality is that Yin is tied to the body, the same way Yang is tied to the mind. Healing is also recursive, like Yin. It moves forward, pauses, and sometimes steps back.

And 2.), Yin is what is needed now to rebalance the world, to give what is needed to heal our ailing planet, along with all its suffering citizenry. Healthy Yin does not seek to hold *all* power, and Yin must have its full share. It does not seek that power for its own sake, as a form of extension of self in the world, it builds power in service of the greater good.

Leadership in Yin times (such as now, when there appear to be so many uncontrollable forces at work) requires giving over to that healing process, not fighting for control, yet doing the Yang work of holding the walls of the container, the context in which one is working, firmly in place, so that Yin, the highly organic and delicate process of rotting and renewing, can take place. Yin/Yang balance in leadership protects the chrysalis, inside of which messy, soupy transformations take place. It then protects the gangly new thing that emerges while it dries its wings and learns to fly.

It is a mistake to think of such leadership as "soft" or "fragile." Just as the so-called "soft skills" of effective communication and relationship-building turn out to be far more challenging for most leaders than the "hard skills" of business literacy, manufacturing prowess or financial wizardry, so leadership in Yin times is where leadership moves from hierarchy and logic (e.g., command and control) to subtle, collaborative, barely visible art form. It is quiet, incremental, gentle and irresistible, much like natural forces such as wind and water erosion. As it says in the ***I Ching,*** "With great leaders, the people say 'We did it ourselves.'"[4]

A clue to the power of Yin can be found in the work on chaos or complexity theory that has evolved in the last thirty years. Acknowledging that the hard sciences cover a very limited portion of reality, mathematicians began to look at the rest of it. Chaos theory is defined by Wikipedia as "states of dynamical systems[5] whose apparently-random states of disorder and irregularities are often governed by deterministic laws that are highly sensitive to initial conditions." In other words, tiny differences at the beginning can have improbably large consequences later on. Those tiny differences lie in the domain of Yin--what lies below the surface and initially can only be sensed or intuited.

Sleep is Yin. Only with our eyes closed and our bodies at rest can we compost the day's experiences, and make meaning of them. When we go to sleep with a question, we usually wake up with an answer, though it may take a few nights. Through our dreams, we assemble fragments of the days, juxtapose them differently and slowly come to new awarenesses, new understandings.

Children, in a growth spurt, often sleep deeply and wake up visibly different--physically, intellectually and/or emotionally. It is a trip to the Yin well of growth. Adults who default to not sleeping in order to "stay caught up" in the rat race are depriving themselves of critical Yin time. And growth.

Learning is Yin. In our Yang world, we often think of learning as the collection of information, of knowledge. We don't recognize that, until knowledge is in the body, until it exists as muscle memory and neural pathway, until the meandering pathway of our vagal nerve can recognize safety in every part of us, we haven't really *learned* something. Because we don't have access to it when it matters. At critical moments, we default instead to our oldest (and often least useful) patterns, the ones we learned as children in order to survive.

Learning requires a willingness to "not know." In our Yang world, not having all the answers is not acceptable, but if you have all the answers, what is there to learn? Your growth will be stunted. The capacity to unlearn, to let go of past answers to discover new ones, to let go of the need to have answers at all and be willing to live in the questions is a Yin capacity.

Forgiveness is Yin. Forgiveness, too, lives in the body. When the body has unclenched, when the body no longer holds resentment and fear, then forgiveness has truly happened. It cannot happen without a descent into the darkness, a composting of feelings and ego, stories and anger. Only then can forgiveness become real and return to the light.

Grieving is Yin. Of all human processes, grief may be the most subterranean and least predictable. Grief travels far underground, even when there is evidence of its presence above ground. Grief, composted, becomes the source of new strengths and capabilities. And like all composting, time is required, as well as heat and moisture. At the same time, above ground, grief requires community in order for healing to occur. Grief unshared is grief unresolved. Perhaps successful grieving is a model of perfecting the Yin/Yang balance.[6]

Jazz is Yin. It is the dance between mastery and improvisation, letting go of any notion of what the notes on the score sheet say *should be* to explore what *could be*, giving, with both control and humility, voice to new possibilities and old pain in the same breath. Just as dark-skinned people brought far from their homeland grieved and composted that grief through music, first into the blues, and then into jazz, turning their anger and sorrow into expressions of fierce beauty. It is music built of cooperation, where leadership is shared, and always evolving.[7]

Anger is Yin. The white-hot incandescent rage that overtakes us, the dark fury of Kali, the Hindu Divine Mother goddess who destroys evil forces, the passion to protect what we care about--all that lies in our depths and erupts from them--these are all part of the aspect of Yin that terrifies us the most. Like Sekhmet, the lion-headed Egyptian goddess of war *and* healing, Yin anger is "the healing intelligence of nature,"[8] in service always of justice. It is all that has been repressed, depressed, and oppressed in us, all that must be faced and owned if our voices are to ring true. It all lies hiding in Yin, a root part of who we are.

And ultimately, much of **Love is Yin**. Love is the deep, mysterious force at the root of all meaning-making. Inexplicable, magical, wondrous. Love fills us, feeds us, supports us, comes from our depths and nurtures our souls. Inexhaustible love arising from the dark, over and over, and carrying us into the Light. As magnificent activist and writer Valerie Kaur puts it, "Love is more than a rush of feeling. Love is sweet labor—fierce, bloody, imperfect and life-giving. A choice we make over and over again."[9] Visiting Yin gives us a chance to rest in that love and renew our souls and our beings. Spiritual leader and teacher Jeannie Zandi says to women, "May we rest together as a holy forest of upright, rooted, integrous, sovereign woman-essence, shining and grounded, ready to take our place at the table."[10]

What then might be the shadow sides of Yin? One shadow is that underground can mean under-handed–sneaky, hidden manipulation of both facts and feelings, attempting to get things accomplished without respecting others' dignity. Another shadow can be passivity, a refusal to take responsibility for making one's way in the world, while martyring oneself in the name of (unhealthy) caretaking. We will explore this question in more detail as we explore maturity and how it works.

---

[1] ***Webster's Illustrated Contemporary Dictionary, Encyclopedic Version,*** 1999, p. 859

[2] Stone, Merlin, ***Ancient Mirrors of Womanhood***, p. 26

[3]Zandi, Jeannie ***Bliss & Grit*** podcast interview "Embodying Yin; A Conversation With Jeannie Zandi," 10/16/2018

[4] Marshall, Lisa, *"Where are the Grownups? Developing Mature Leaders"* chapter ***in 2006 Pfeiffer Annual on Training***, p. 217

[5] human beings, for example

[6] Kaur, op. cit., pp. 33-64

[7] Thanks to Srinija Srinivasan for this insight!

[8] Nicki Scully, ***Sekhmet; Transformation in the Belly of the Goddess***, p. 15

[9] Kaur, op. cit., p. 278

[10] www.facebook.com/notes/the-work-of-jeannie-zandi/woman-crowned/1803519259706335/

Your Story

1. Reading this, what was your reaction? Was it scary? Self-evident? Enticing? Did it produce relief? Anxiety? Neither or both? Write a few sentences about what you experienced in your body as you read these words.

2. Contemplating this description, what parts of your story include experiencing/exploring Yin? What parts haven't yet, but probably should?

3. What about Yin scares you the most? What draws you to it?

4. How balanced between Yin and Yang do you feel you currently are? What might you do to improve that balance?

Chapter Three: What Then is Yang?

Let's be clear: I am describing healthy Yang, not the vastly unhealthy version that is inundating us these days.

Healthy Yang builds growing out of healthy Yin. It takes a need to make a mark on the world and turns it into beauty and stability--be it a bridge, a book, a building or a business. Healthy Yang is active--it climbs, runs, dives, explores, using the real world to come to understand itself better. It gets things done. Healthy Yang knows that its gift of focus can be over-utilized, and remembers to periodically broaden its perspective. Even when healthy Yang has a well-developed and specific body of knowledge, it is always curious about how the parts interrelate with the whole.

Healthy Yang is not afraid of tenderness. It knows that kindness and strength dance together, that size and stature are not the same thing, and that a disciplined mind combined with a disciplined body has a beauty all its own. It makes available the whole gamut of human emotions and is not afraid of any of them. Healthy Yang recognizes that trauma is deeply rooted in humans' long history, and that the responsibility for undoing the resulting fear and constrictions, both emotional and physical, is shared by all. And that, in this moment, it is white people's especial job.

Healthy Yang shows love through service and protection, caring for loved ones and community. Maintenance of buildings, vehicles or organizations can all be acts of healthy Yang, as can playing the role of provider, in a variety of forms. Healthy Yang is very drawn to being "in service."

Healthy Yang is self-aware. It recognizes its impact on its environment, both people and planet, and seeks to ensure that the impact is in service of balance. Healthy Yang loves to learn, and lives inside its questions, without a need to have answers. It uses logic and analysis to solve problems while being careful not to optimize a portion of the whole at the expense of the rest. It recognizes leadership as "stewardship of the whole, not ownership of the parts."[1]

Healthy Yang is humble. It knows it doesn't have all the answers, or even the capacity to see any issue in its entirety. It does not seek fame or stardom, recognizing that those are fundamental symptoms of imbalance. Healthy Yang is comfortable asking for help, and does not need to have subordinates or be in a superior position.

Healthy Yang seeks balance--with Yin, with the natural world and within. It will compete, but only to learn about itself, not to conquer. As Rilke said, in his poem, "The Man Watching," Yang grows *"by being defeated, decisively, by constantly greater beings."* Healthy Yang knows that its roots lie in healthy Yin, and vice versa.

---

[1] Vice-Admiral of Naval Aviation Joseph Dyer, in conversation with author, 19 March, 2002

Your Story

1. Where do you see Yang in your life, your story? Where is it healthy Yang, where is not?

2. What would you say is the balance of Yin and Yang in your life currently? Are you happy with that balance?

3. Describe some of your experiences with healthy and unhealthy Yang, either in yourself or with other people.

4. Think of a time when Yang had you by the "short and curlies." How might you have rebalanced? How did you?

Chapter Four: Where Do We Go? My New Journey

hen I set out to write the first book, I was braiding three threads together: maturity, leadership and story, using the format of the Hero's Journey. I stalled completely when I went to write a chapter called "The Journey." After a while, a tiny, whiny voice appeared inside my head: "Why do we have to take a journey?" it said. "I don't want to take a journey." Completely stymied, I walked around the house for several days, unable to see, hear or feel a way forward.

Finally, as I stared at my blank screen, a much deeper voice said, "Because you're supposed to grow up, dummy!" "Oh right," I thought, "This IS supposed to be a book about leadership maturity!" Humans' profound drive for maturity, wholeness and balance--even crippled as we are by our biases, our history and our fears--moves me deeply. It is one of our most important traits. And it is what it will take to save us from ourselves.

I had originally been looking for a road map, or perhaps, more accurately, a treasure map. I wanted a definition, a clear sense of what maturity looked, sounded and felt like, a clear "X" on the map of life. I remember my shock upon discovering that, in the 90's, there was very little literature to be found on the subject. It was as if the world had, by consensus, agreed that we would know it when we saw it, so it didn't need to be discussed. I felt I had stumbled on a hole in our thinking the size of the Grand Canyon.

Yes, philosophers (mostly male) had pontificated on "character" and such for a long time, but no one had really sat down to define maturity itself. So I conducted interviews (60+) and did my own research.

Originally, I identified the four domains of maturity as emotional, intellectual, moral and spiritual. I now choose differently: the four domains are physical, emotional, intellectual and spiritual. I do this for three reasons: a.) a recognition that morality works best distributed in all domains, b.) I've been exploring the work of many brilliant healers who study how, as Bessel Van der Kolk says, "the body keeps the score," recognizing how deeply saturated our culture is with trauma issues and c.) reading Chellis Glendinning and my study of the First Nations' cosmology, the Medicine Wheels, let me see that our relationship with the physical world is a critical piece of maturity--and a path to it.

I have settled on the terms Yin and Yang, because it seems dangerous to even use the terms female and male, masculine and feminine, given our hyper-gendered society and the violence with which current discussions of every individual's right to a place in the world is being conducted. Because this language is less familiar, perhaps it will allow readers to see that these distinctions all exist on a spectrum, a continuum. Most all of us fall somewhere other than the extreme ends of that spectrum. Every good leader I've ever coached was good as much or more because of their Yin qualities as for their Yang abilities to get things done. Ultimately, the goal of the Journey--the goal of life--for every human being is to become whole, and thus to balance both Yin and Yang in ways that work for them, their lives, their context.

Your Story

1. Think of a time when you had Yin and Yang in balance. Describe it in detail. What allowed that to happen?

2. How have you thought about maturity, the need to "grow up," or "adulting"? Has it been part of your story? How does it show up? Is it scary or attractive or both?

3. How has the instinctive drive for wholeness shown up in your life? Describe times it has manifested and times it has been defeated.

4. Off the top of your head, which domains of maturity do you think you're strongest in? Weakest? (There will be more exploration of this later.)

Chapter Five: Where Do We Take This?

In *The Hero With a Thousand Faces,* Campbell claims that the great stories have the same fundamental architecture, which he calls "The Hero's Journey." In the Yang Hero's journey, external accomplishment is the primary focus. The goal ultimately is to return a "boon" to the community--give the gift one had been seeking, either as a trophy or other significant accomplishment. To do this, one will have received some sort of "call," set off on a journey during which allies and monsters are discovered, the goal is achieved and the gift brought back to one's community.

The Yin leadership Journey, whether you identify as male or female or non-binary or trans, is the same *and* it is different. There is a call, a path to travel, monsters and allies, and gifts to bring to the community. However, Yin Journeys are circular, spiral, elliptical, and often about overcoming through cunning and caring. Where Yang sets a plan and tries to execute it, Yin strategy is fluid and emergent, built of small moves.[1] It is also an exploration of darkness, the darkness that comes with dissolution of ego and giving over to what is. It requires learning to rest in the darkness, rather than fight it.

While the sword of discernment may yet be needed, and the return to Light can be momentarily blinding, the Yin Journey explores a different set of allies and monsters and a different path to balance and wholeness than the Yang Journey. Yin leaders do confront monsters, but more often thru their willingness to "tend and befriend," coupled with a brave curiosity that Jeannie Zandi models by her "Hey friend, what's up? Why are you behaving this way?"[2] response to harassment.

The Yin Journey has been more actively being explored in recent decades, yet its application to leadership maturity is still fertile territory for discussion and exploration. My focus will be on the "Crone stage", elderhood, the ultimate developmental phase of Yin life, as this is the domain of maturity. If we plan on living, we have no choice but to arrive here chronologically. The real question is, can we arrive here in our hearts, our minds, our spirits *and* our bodies? That has always been the maturity challenge, and it is especially salient in these dark times......... What I've come to understand is that Yin is the source of the growth that makes maturity possible. Yin *is* the power in the leadership journey, the source of our voice and our ability to act.

So what are the specific qualities of this kind of maturity? Using Robert Kegan's ***The Evolving Self,*** I identify them as a looping journey around and between our two fundamental developmental pulls. One pull is our Yang need for autonomy, which, at its most mature, manifests as a vast and fearless curiosity with its concurrent ability to separate and name. The other pull is our Yin need for connection, which, evolved, becomes a great capacity for love in all its forms, rooted in a capacity for seeing the inter-connectedness of everything. The developmental dilemma in these times is that robust maturity requires both, yet we've privileged Yang over Yin to a terrifying degree.

From the very beginning, even as children, healthy development requires that we balance our autonomy and connection. "Along with the maturing of individuation [autonomy] comes the maturing of our ability for intimacy with another person [connection]" writes Judith Blackstone, author and psychotherapist[3]. One could think of these dynamics as knitting needles, knitting a whole person together. However, because this process is so often interrupted, and stitches dropped, we rarely manage to grow up balanced and whole.

In his book ***Nature and Madness,*** pioneering ecologist Paul Shepard pointed out nearly four decades ago that humans evolved in this dance between autonomy and connection over millions of years within a matrix--the natural world--with which we have largely lost relationship. That matrix offered (and required) a clear progression of explorations and relations: Knowing one's mother and kin, knowing the animals, knowing the plants, knowing one's waters, deserts and mountains, knowing the stars. All of that had to be known, absorbed, and comprehended in order to mature. It was (and is) the responsibility of the elders to oversee this process:

> *"Their goal is not to perpetuate the prenatal subjective merge state but, in a staircase of mergers and departures, to identify a self (or selves: a resolution of the inchoate "we," "they," and "it" as well as "I"), leading to a more mature sense of relatedness. In this way a good sense of being in the cosmos is the result of two decades of timed events that involve the person with others and with the nonhuman in an extraordinary interplay."*[4]

My quest now is: define what that identified sense of self, a more mature sense of relatedness, might look like for all of us in the 21st century. What might its implications be for the way we live our lives? And for how we develop as leaders?

In service of that work, I've set the current context for this writing in the spring and summer of 2020. Next, I define what I mean by "finding one's voice." I'll explore what constitutes Yin maturity in four separate domains or "Directions"~physical, emotional, intellectual and spiritual.

I also explore the notion of Monsters~the beliefs, experiences, stories and events that cripple us, prevent us from reaching our fullest potential. Everyone has their own set of Monsters (aka, "our demons") and there are whole constellations of them embedded in the world at large. Facing Monsters down is a critical part of every human's journey. In that context, I'll look at what leadership is and how Yin leadership is different.

Then I'll answer the important question of how the Yin Journey to maturity is different from the Yang Journey. I offer some archetypes that support the Yin Journey and how they function as our allies. Finally, I move into a conversation about elderhood as the final stage of maturity, why it matters and how it might be experienced. The last section, "Future Perfect," invites you to an experience of a very different world, one that holds Yin and Yang in healthy balance. Explore it, try it on, and begin your own journey of imagining how the world could and should be.

---

[1] brown, adrienne maree, ***Emergent Strategy***, p.23

[2] Zandie, op. cit.

[3] Blackstone, Judith, ***Trauma and the Unbound Body***, p. 12

[4] Shepard, Paul, ***Nature and Madness.*** p. 110

Your Story

1. As you think about your story, what are some moments where you can clearly point to Yang-style accomplishment, where you "caught the ball," or "brought back the Golden Fleece," the talisman of success.

2. Can you describe some moments in your story that required a more Yin approach, where you had to learn to "rest in the darkness," the not-knowing, in order to make progress?

3. Under stress, do you revert to Yang? Or Yin? Do you know the source of that impulse? What story do you tell yourself?

4. Moving from autonomy to connection and back again requires a very Yin experience of, for a moment, or for a period or time, not knowing who you are or where you are resting. There is an identity reset every time we make that transition. This is most visible in little children, who alternate periods of exploring and testing with periods of integrating and resting. Think of some times in your adult life when you have been in transition from your connection self to your autonomy self, or vice versa, and describe the felt sense of that.

Chapter Six: What do I mean by "Finding One's Voice?"

> *"Once upon a time, when women were birds, there*
> *was the simple understanding that to sing at dawn*
> *and to sing at dusk was to heal the world through joy.*
> *The birds still remember what we have forgotten,*
> *that the world is meant to be celebrated."*
> *Terry Tempest Williams,* [1]

t the personal level, our celebration initially takes form as the ability to embody our entire self, to *be* the celebration, fearlessly and fully, as children do. It means joyously owning ourselves and the world around us and celebrating it in all its messy glory. It means recognizing that all "knowing" starts with being grounded--in one's body, and in the earth herself. When that happens, it often means being the channel through which the Earth, Mother Nature, Gaia speaks. When we make the Yin side heard, Gaia is heard.

It is no accident that women figure so prominently in the "green movements" that are blossoming all over the world. When women find their voices, their voices are in service--the land, Mother Earth, Mother Nature, Gaia--the places where their roots grow, the places where they have connected to the land. Voices of the natural world, from Dorothy Wordsworth, Gene Stratton-Porter, Rachel Carson, Gretel Erlich, Annie Dillard, and Terry Tempest Williams, to Robin Wall Kimmerer, Sharon Blackie,

Louise Erdrich, Mary Oliver, Diana Beresford-Kroeger and so many more, all speak from and for the land, the planet.

Finding our voice can be learning to articulate the questions one's soul is grappling with as well as the current state (even if disordered) of our thinking and feeling about the answers. Beyond that, it may be the willingness to make both the questions and their answers public, to "give yoice" to them. Another way to say it: speaking the questions around which we are currently organizing our lives, the questions we have historically avoided and are perhaps now ready to face, and the questions our future is drawing us towards. Sharing those questions with others. Recognizing that it is okay if our answers are imperfect.

Finding our voice includes claiming our sovereignty, our right to have choice and to have intention in the world, in the ways *we* choose. Until we have our independence, we cannot successfully be interdependent. In a sense, it is a privileging of the right side of our brains (loosely described as the creative, sensing part of our brain) over the left (the logical, analytical part). Ian McGilchrist, author of ***The Master and His Emissary***, says

> *I believe the essential difference between the right hemisphere and the left hemisphere is that the right hemisphere pays attention to the Other: to what it is that exists apart from ourselves, with which it sees itself in profound relation....By contrast, the left hemisphere pays attention to the virtual world that it has created, which is self-consistent but self-contained, ultimately disconnected from the Other, making it*

> *powerful-but also curiously impotent, because it is ultimately only able to operate on, and to know, itself."*[2]

It is fascinating to contemplate that the motor speech center (though not all of language) exists in the left hemisphere, giving it greater power to articulate its explicit wishes, even as it is "unrealistically positive in its self-appraisal."[3] No wonder the claiming of our sovereignty is such a challenging Journey. We give voice to that which is implicit, relational, sensed and unexplained!

At base, all of this implies a profound "knowing," one that comes from our body, not our mind. This somatic knowing represents the accumulation of *all* our intelligences, a deeply felt sense of what our truths are and what is right for us. Finding our voice means using that knowing to make clear our conditions of satisfaction when we make requests of others. And it is the result of a deep series of interior journeys, (willingly or unwillingly taken), journeys that require facing the monsters of our own making as well as the very real ones in the external world.

It is important to note that, in the Yin form of voice, our "way of being" in the world can reflect our voice as much as the words we choose. It is whatever form of self-expression fits the person we are, from someone who heals with their hands to someone who creates art or music or sews or cooks or starts businesses or raises children or sets legal precedents. All these activities are forms of "voice," along with how we dress or what our home looks like, or where we volunteer. Anything that reflects our celebration of the world, and our recognition of our ties to it is a form of voice.

When women do their voice-finding, they often do it collectively, as the Women in White did when they brought down dictator Charles Taylor's regime in Liberia, or the Grandmothers of the Plaza del Mayo when they insisted on finding their "disappeared" children and grandchildren in Argentina, Uruguay and Chile. Earlier generations here in the U.S. had churches, sewing circles, knitting groups and quilting bees as ways to come together. Today, for many, our voices have been found in the form of #MeToo. Giving voice to what matters to us is how we build community. And as noted author and MD Rachel Remen clarifies in several videos, "community is essential for healing." For Yin, community is life-giving.

Finding our voice in one domain of life, however, doesn't guarantee that we have found it in all of them. For example, we can be spiritually mature and can still be quite immature emotionally, giving those around us constant whiplash. Human beings are built for balance; finding a consistent voice or way of being that rests in love in the emotional, intellectual, spiritual and physical realms is the Holy Grail for women. That kind of maturity creates the human beings the rest of us look at and want to emulate when we grow up!

---

[1] Williams, Terry Tempest, ***When Women Were Birds***, *p. 225*
[2] McGilchrist, Iain, ***Ways of Attending, How Our Divided Brain Constructs the World,*** p. 23
[3] Ibid, p.21

Your Story

1. How do you "celebrate the world"? Does it feel like you are "giving voice" to what really matters when you do it?

2. When do you feel most like you are speaking with your authentic voice? How often do you find that it is rooted in love of and protection of the Earth, Gaia, Mother Nature?

3. When you are most certain that you "know" something, where does that live in your body? How is it experienced? Describe it in detail.

4. What have been some significant experiences of collective voice-finding for you? Was it surprising to find that others shared your concerns or thoughts? Was your voice strengthened by that discovery?

Chapter Seven: Defining Yin Maturity

Let's start with defining maturity itself: what *is* it and why does it matter? Webster's usefully defines *mature* as, among other things, "fully developed in character and powers."[1] As to why it matters, Elisabet Sahtouris, evolutionary biologist, notes sadly "humans are a desert-making species." She observes the world in terms of maturation cycles and has seen over and over that "creative cooperation is the mature way in evolution. It's cheaper to feed your enemies than to kill them." The result? "It is time for us now to be a desert *greening* species."[2] Time to grow up.

In the past 5000 years, we've turned our understanding of maturity on its head from the one Paul Shepard describes. We've labeled "primitive" or "mystical" anyone who is connected to a bigger world, to the planet as a living organism. We've labeled "civilized" those whose lives are utterly disconnected from that matrix in which our species evolved.

Many ancient teaching traditions--the Native American Medicine Wheels, the Celts, Buddhism's samsara, Ayurveda, the Tao, and most indigenous cultures--teach us that life is a circle of death and Rebirth. There are journeys within journeys in that circle, each journey requiring and resulting in balancing Yin and Yang, masculine and feminine. As the Medicine Wheels teach, we each must travel in the four directions, representing, in the North, Wisdom and Knowledge, in the West, Introspection and

Intuition, in the South, Trust and Innocence and in the East, Illumination and Enlightenment:

> *At birth, each of us is given a particular Beginning Place within these Four Great Directions on the Medicine Wheel. This starting place gives us our First way of Perceiving. Throughout our lives this remains our easiest and most natural Way of interacting with our World. However, if we remain where we were born, we will atrophy and die.*
>
> *For example, those possessing only the Seeing of the North will be Wise, but they can also be detached from Feeling. Those who attempt to live only in the East will have clear, farsighted Vision, but they also will never be close to things. Such people will feel separated, above Life, and will never understand that they can be touched by Life.*
>
> *Those who perceive only from the West will go over the same thoughts again and again in their minds, and yet will always be undecided. And if people insist upon dwelling in the idyllic Innocence of the South, they will pretend their lives long and find only disappointment.*
>
> *There are people who work hard to develop the Powers of all Four Directions. They will discover the satisfaction of knowing the Self and seeing Life as more than an abstract concept or simple belief.*[3]

To do that work, to balance ourselves in all domains and know Life fully, we must do our Yin work. We must take an inner journey within each of those directions, touching on each of the four points again, through the specific focus of that lens.

Until we, as a species, achieve the kind of maturity that supports creative cooperation, until we can balance ourselves in both character and powers, until we can honor both Yin and Yang consistently, we cannot--and will not--move ourselves out of the nightmare scenarios of crisis after crisis that now afflict us. What follows are my efforts to delineate more precisely and fully what true maturity looks, sounds and feels like. I cover both its autonomy and connection aspects, in each of four domains (or directions)--the physical, the emotional, the intellectual and the spiritual. And I explore the Monsters that impede our development in each Direction.

---

[1] ***Webster's Illustrated Contemporary Dictionary, Encyclopedic Edition***, p. 445

[2] https://www.youtube.com/watch?v=n1mvI2hEzlA

[3] Storm, Hyemeyohsts, ***Lightningbolt***, pp.201-202

Yin Maturity – the Physical

s I've explored the Native American cosmology of the Medicine Wheels, I've come to understand them as a brilliant and sophisticated world view and maturity model, arguably the best I have discovered in thirty years of thinking about the subject. In that model, the natural world, and our relationship to it are profoundly important. The Wheels have not lost sight of the world in which and for which we evolved.[1]

In my earlier work, I did not explicitly include kinesthetic, somatic or physical awareness, embedding it in other places. Since then, I've explored many aspects of the explosion in body/nature awareness, somatic practices and mindfulness practices. I've come to see that, in many ways, this awareness is actually the starting point for all of us. The physical-being in our bodies, on this planet-is where and how we evolved, in balance with the natural world, the place where we were once always at home and part of something larger, a connection we have largely lost.

In the run-up to modern life, we've lost access to that which we had, in essence, been designed for, the matrix in which we had been grown. We've lost relationship to that which we had known for thousands of generations-a Yin/Yang balanced relationship to the earth. We have come, instead, to live in what has become, slowly and inexorably, an increasingly alien environment (which Sharon Blackie describes in ***If Women Rose Rooted*** quite accurately as "the Wasteland"). From this "original trauma,"[2] equivalent to ripping a baby from its mother's breast, humans have now created 300 generations' worth of repeating or increasing trauma.

When we lived as hunter-gathers, as many anthropologists have observed, there was actually far less work and far more time for celebration than there is today.[3] Embedded in the matrix of the natural world, knowing always how to find food, water and shelter, we were safe, and secure. We had wholeness. We could glory in creation. Elisabet Sahtouris likes to say, "We communed, instead of communicating."[4] We were

> *"conscious and in contact with ourselves everywhere in our body,...experiencing ourselves as undivided consciousness, a subtle, unified ground of consciousness, pervading our whole body and our environment...our thoughts, emotions, sensations and perceptions occur(ring) as a unity...alive and responsive to the world around us."* [5]

We were, quite literally, *in touch.*

Our estrangement from the natural world is now nearly complete, as we can see in so many children who can only encounter life mediated through devices. Designed biologically as we are for serotonin, the chemical that naturally keeps us calmly alert, present and positive, we've become addicted instead to the dopamine surges provided by our increasingly powerful and invasive electronic devices. We're not designed for constant dopamine hits, and it costs us physiologically. [6] As Chellis Glendinning noted presciently in the 1990's,

> *"Original trauma is the disorientation we experience, however consciously or unconsciously, because we do not live in the natural. It is the psychic displacement, the exile that is inherent in civilized life. It is our homelessness."* [7]

While the reasons for the transition from hunter-gatherer lifestyles to agricultural and pastoral may never be totally clear, the results are:

> *"The human relationship to the natural world was gradually changed from respect for and participation in its elliptical wholeness to one of detachment, management, control, and finally domination."*[8]

Much of the Medicine Wheels' power as a maturity model has to do with the way the Wheels recognize/restore/reinforce a balance of nature and human activity, how they reflect the hunter-gatherer recognition that all life has equal value--plants, animals, humans, the planet. With a carefully thought-out system of checks and balances (copied to some degree by the Founding Fathers to design balance into the U. S. system of government), no decision is made until it is vetted by all those affected. At its finest, this slow process consistently restores the Yin/Yang balance and never allows power to concentrate too fully in one place.

So what are the specific qualities of someone with Yin Physical Maturity? On the **Connection/Love** side, maturity starts with being deeply at home in one's body, *however that body may be*. It recognizes that the brain/body split is a false dichotomy, and listens closely to the gut/heart messages that those parts of the brain send through the vagal nervous system. It includes the discipline to maintain some degree of fitness, and an ability to acknowledge a changing body over time. It is what loving oneself looks like.

And then we extend that love to the world around us. We have some understanding of our place in the web of livingness that is Planet Earth. Our physical senses of stability, resilience, and balance affect our willingness to explore. They allow us to know our carrying capacity and adjust accordingly, including knowing when to explore and reach out, when to stand, when to run, when to hide, when to befriend or tend. In other words, how to *be* in this exquisite world.

On the **Autonomy/Curiosity** side, it is our sensing relation with our inner and outer worlds. It begins with our sensing relation within ourselves (critical to finding our voice is sensing its first stirrings within us), then an awareness of the impact of our presence on others. Then it extends to the biological world, familiarity with one's ecosystem at micro and macro levels.

The body is where we find our voice. It requires being centered in our ventral vagal nervous system, that part of us which supports the sense of safety that enables healthy social engagement. If we are trapped in fight, flight or freeze, we cannot actually listen, we can only sort for signs of danger. [9] In a way, this is all about listening--to ourselves, to our loved ones, to our communities, and to the natural world around us. Indeed, truly effective listening requires the tiniest muscle in the human body--the stapedius--to register and respond to changes in frequency. A sense of safety is required for that to happen. Listening is a fundamentally physical act! As Ursula Le Guin wisely notes, "Body is story; voice tells it."[10]

What gets in our way, what inhibits the kinds of love and curiosity we're talking about? What are the **Monsters** that must be encountered and tamed? First and foremost is Cartesian duality, the mind-body split propagated in the last five centuries, and powerfully reinforced in the last 40 years by the silicon-based technology proliferation. Before that, there were the ways agriculture evolved from working with nature to seeking to manage and control it. That evolution led to disconnection from the wild matrix we evolved in and for which we are designed.

And then there are, of course, always the potential realities of the aging process--gravity winning, energy ebbing, health issues, isolation and resignation--none of which are written in stone. Additionally, living in a society stuck in stages of adolescence it can't move beyond because of this disconnection, with its resulting negative views on aging and death (along with its rejection of the power of elderhood) constitute a potent set of monsters to face.

Finally, there is Western society's fear of Yin itself--fear of the feminine, of darkness, of decay, of dying, of "not knowing"--all critical elements of a healthy living cycle. We've medicalized dying in our search for "more life," such that, while we're living longer, we're also living sicker, more depressed and without joy or celebration.[11] Without a sense of connection to our ancestors, death seems final and empty, not part of a cycle where we can pass on wisdom and role model grace. If we knew we belonged here, we would know we were part of something larger. As a continent of--willing or otherwise--immigrants, (all but the original peoples left their ancestors behind), that disconnection and loss further increases our inability to face death.

---

[1] Unsurprising, given that it reflects a view of maturity derived from living in the natural world, the one for which we are built

[2] Glendinning, Chellis, ***My Name is Chellis Glendinning and I am in Recovery From Western Civilization***, p.64

[3] https://www.shelterwoodforestfarm.com/blog/the-lost-forest-gardens-of-europe?fbclid=IwAR2nt4PwacB4w
RnB6JDpdG0rxaVPAkpiwg5V2Yp4iemRqFLQ7Kn0Ecviw1o

[4] Sahtouris, Elisabet, ***The Secret to Human Coexisting,*** Big Speak Speakers Bureau, You Tube, April 20, 2016

[5] Blackstone, op. cit., p.1

[6] Author conversation with neuroscience expert Janet Crawford, 3/20

[7] Glendinning, op. cit., p. 64

[8] Ibid, p.70

[9] Rosenberg, Stanley, ***Accessing the Healing Power of the Vagus Nerve***, p. 167

[10] Le Guin, Ursula K., the wave in the mind, p. 288

[11] Jenkinson, Stephen, ***Die Wise,*** pp. 132-33

Your Story

1. As you read about the Connection/Love aspect of Yin Physical Maturity, what comes up for you? Is this way of being at home in oneself something that draws you? Describe a time when you think you achieved that kind of at-home-ness.

2. On the Autonomy/Curiosity side, how would you describe yourself? How familiar are you with yourself, with your environment, with your ecosystem?

3. Which of the Monsters that inhibit/prevent physical maturity show up in your story? How? Are there others not mentioned? Give examples.

4. As you think about this form of maturity, what draws you to it? What repels you? How would you describe your relationship to it?

Yin Maturity – Intellectual

t is ironic that intellectual maturity is the most highly privileged, explored, researched and written about form of maturity, (and in many cases, the only form of maturity people recognize or have thought about). If the physical and emotional are the most Yin of the maturities, this is the most Yang.

Intellectual maturity however, has unique biological (hence Yin) requirements. It requires both a healthy pre-frontal cortex and access to one's ventral vagal nervous system (the part of the vagal system that supports effective social interaction) to effectively process information and make good decisions. Neurological research indicates that, to a greater or lesser degree, today most of us have pre-frontal cortexes that are damaged or never got fully developed. In crisis times, it's all too easy to get knocked down the ladder of nervous functioning to fight or flight, and even to freeze.[1]

So what does the **Connection/Love** form of Yin intellectual maturity look, sound and feel like? It is a willingness to engage with others whose ideas are different, along with the capacity to connect the dots, to see underlying/overarching patterns and then weave the parts into whole. It is a sensitive weighing of the relational moral voice (Yin) and the absolute moral voice (Yang), in ways that both feel acknowledged.[2] Yin feels wonder, the curiosity about the potential for *more* and *different.* It addresses the four directions with both care and kindness, working towards learning and cooperation, rather than towards amassing wealth and/or power.

And on the **Autonomy/Curiosity** side? Well, if Yang organizes, systematizes, and Gets Things Done, Yin intellectual curiosity explores and grows organically, messily, chaotically, until suddenly there is a whole new something there. Yin feels its way into the big picture and then can put everything in a place where it works best. Yin's vast curiosity results in questions that are often very different and far-ranging. For example:

- Janine Benyus's "What if we looked at how nature has already solved most of our problems?";
- Elinor Ostrom's "Was the 'Tragedy of the Commons' (an economic assumption that humans could never share resources) always true?";
- Elisabet Sahtouris's "What does the maturation phase that we see in biological evolution look like in human beings?";
- Kate Raworth's "What about a model of the economy that reflects reality?"; or
- Courtney Martin's "How do we redefine 'better off' for the 21st century?"

Yin autonomy can comfortably hold competing ideas, in part because of a deep willingness to face reality, and from that reality develop whole new possibilities. Where Yang curiosity has been captured by the notions that growth equals making money and that more is better, Yin curiosity wonders about other ways to grow, to have or be "more." Yin curiosity wants to *learn.*

What are the **Monsters** that impede Yin intellectual maturity? Fear of insufficiency is a big one: "oh, my ideas can't possibly be useful or good." "They'll laugh at me." "I don't know enough." Another monster is all that, in both nature and nurture, results in damage to the prefrontal cortex or restriction in the vagal nervous system. This may range from nutritional deficiencies to parental deficiencies. Similarly, trauma constrictions can form a constellation of monsters that prevent Yin intellectual maturity by shrinking our worlds into tiny pieces, preventing a big picture view. Yang likes to make us feel as though the questions we're asking don't have enough rigor and discipline, rather than accepting that they are simply unconventional, and, hence, unsettling.

---

[1] Dana, Deb, ***Polyvagal Theory in Therapy, Engaging the Rhythm of Regulation,*** pp. 9-14
[2] Carol Gilligan, ***In a Different Voice,*** sfonline.barnard.edu/sfxxx/documents/gilligan.pdf

Your Story

1. As you read about the Connection/Love aspect of Yin Intellectual Maturity, what comes up for you? Based on your experiences, does the idea that Intellectual Maturity has biological requirements make sense? Describe a time when you think you were able to see patterns, connect the dots and see a whole picture rooted in your sense of wonder.

2. On the Autonomy/Curiosity side, how would you describe yourself? Do you think of yourself as a learner? Do you find you sometimes ask questions that surprise others? Give some examples of yourself in this domain.

3. Which of the Monsters that inhibit/prevent intellectual maturity show up in your story? How? Are there others not mentioned? Give examples.

4. As you think about this form of maturity, what draws you to it? What repels you? How would you describe your relationship to it?

Yin Maturity - Emotional

Since the mid-1980s, Paul Ray and Sherry Anderson, researchers at Stanford, have been tracking the growth of a demographic they call "Cultural Creatives," people who value the environment, democracy, sustainability and compassion, amongst other things.[1] Interestingly, the numbers of people who identify that way has been growing steadily, despite the lack of representation of those values in the media. (As a side effect, almost all of them feel isolated for caring as they do.) In 1999, Cultural Creatives were 26% of the population. In 2008, they were nearly 35% of the population, [2] and it's now estimated that they may be half the population in the U.S. and Europe.[3] I take that as an indicator that Yin emotional maturity is actually a growing phenomenon. Cultural Creatives run 60% female, 40% male.

Emotional intelligence and maturity in general have come into their own as a concept in the last three decades, widely written about, explored, discussed, and frankly, resisted. In fact, one could argue that the rising tide of nationalism and narrow-mindedness across the globe is a function of resentment at being asked to be self-aware and compassionate. Arlie Hochschild's book, ***Strangers in Their Own Land***, argues that the deepest resentment those on the right feel is around being told what to *feel*--that they should care about people other than their own tribe.[4]

Poet and philosopher David Whyte, on the other hand, often speaks of "a profound ability to make ourselves large enough, brave enough and generous enough for the triumphs and profound difficulties needed to live even the most ordinary human life." That serves nicely as a descriptive container for Yin emotional maturity.

What then are the qualities of emotionally mature Yin **Connection/Love?** Judith Blackstone describes mature love this way: "love that does not require us to make sacrifices of essential parts of our humanness, such as our ability for independent, original thought, or our love for other people outside of the spiritual path." [5] That kind of mature connection results in a capacity to affiliate, to sustain loving relationships with others and with the world. It includes an innate sense of "fairness," rooted in affection and affiliation. At its highest level, I find it similar to good mothering: it offers the capacity to undertake sustained responsibility for others, including making and living with irreversible moral choices.[6] At the same time, it is the ability to hold anxiety without collapsing while making the same request of others; to hold boundaries and self-differentiate without losing connection[7].

Emotionally mature Yin **Autonomy/Curiosity** often takes an unorthodox view of the world, rather than Yang's linear extrapolation. Its view of reality includes the seen and the unseen. Its favorite questions are "what if?" and "what more?" Such curiosity has agency--the ability to self-authorize[8]--to give oneself permission to explore, ask the unasked questions and give voice to unsettling points of view or concerns. It also fuels the ability to know ourselves intimately, overcoming the fear that we will be found wanting by ourselves if we delve too deeply.

And what are the **Monsters,** what makes it hard to achieve Yin emotional maturity? Monsters start with the lack of role models in our lives, where instead of true adult behavior from our caregivers, we often see narcissism, the need to be right, apathy, insecurity, or anger. Very often fear and childhood survival techniques taught us that fawning or placating was the safest route and we default to them as adults. The Yin desire to "tend and befriend," (the feminine addition to "fight or flight" reactions) can also devolve into accepting abuse. If we weren't taken seriously as children, it may lead to trivializing our own feelings and insights, believing them to be of no value.

---

[1] Ray & Anderson, ***The Cultural Creatives: How 50 Million People Are Changing the World***

[2] http://culturalcreatives.org/cultural-creatives/

[3] https://www.huffpost.com/entry/cultural-creatives-are-ch_b_9857452

[4] Airlie Hochschild, ***Strangers in Their Own Land, Anger and Mourning on the American Right*** 2016 Kindle version location 3664

[5] Blackstone, op. cit., p. 124

[6] Marshall, ***Speak the Truth and Point to Hope: The Leader's Journey to Maturity,*** p. 14

[7] Ibid, p. 145.

[8] Expression learned from Prof. Carol Stoneburner, my daughters' teacher at Guilford College

Your Story

1. As you read about the Connection/Love aspect of Yin Emotional Maturity, what comes up for you? Is the concept of sustaining relationships something that draws you? Describe a time when you think you were able to hold anxiety without collapsing, to self-differentiate without losing connection.

2. On the Autonomy/Curiosity side, how would you describe yourself? How able to "self-authorize" are you, or is fear of losing other's high opinion/respect more important?

3. Which of the Monsters that inhibit/prevent Emotional Maturity show up in your story? How? Are there others not mentioned? Give examples.

4. As you think about this form of maturity, what draws you to it? What repels you? How would you describe your relationship to it?

Yin Maturity - Spiritual

he Yin spiritual journey is significantly different than the Yang. Yin spirituality is diffuse, permeable and immanent, not the driven, almost scalding desire to connect to the Divine often associated with Yang spirituality. Deeply felt Yin spirituality often takes the form of ongoing gratitude and compassion, a loving kindness directed at oneself as well as others. Yin spirituality (like Yin work) is a way of being *while* doing. This is because, as my colleague Karen Lam notes, "the Yin has a sophistication about energy, the invisible fabric between us, that the Yang doesn't, as it focuses on what is visible."

In Yin, the mature emotional **Connection/Love** qualities begin with an ability to offer loving kindness to oneself, to one's loved ones, and ultimately to the world ***as it is***. This is a very different daily practice than "sitting on the cushion" for hours on end, the traditionally rigorous Yang meditation practice. It is, instead, accessing the "felt sensing" of our bodies to heal undigested feelings while honoring the Holy. It extends into a deep desire to utilize and return the gifts life has offered, connection to a larger whole and to Source. Because it frequently shows up as a gentle infusion of immanent Spirit into all one does--"work is love made visible"[1]--it is frequently dismissed as somehow "unspiritual", not really rigorous enough to indicate one has a committed spiritual life.

However, Yin spiritual maturity's faith in the human spirit, in its ability to be and do good, is at the root of what has come to be known as Servant Leadership, as described by John Greenleaf. Servant Leadership concepts may be the first introduction to Yin spiritual maturity that Yang leaders have--and the notion that humility, service and kindness are critical leadership attributes is very often "new news!"

Mature spiritual Yin **Autonomy/Curiosity** takes many forms. Stillness or other forms of listening practices that enable discernment of where Spirit is leading can be great enablers of maturity. The ability to explore without judgment, and then to practice surrender to what is has a particularly Yin quality. To ask "what does Spirit want of me?" or as author Meg Wheatley said in March, 2020, "What is the work that needs doing? Am I in position to do it?" is to set ego aside and face reality head on. That ability to refocus from "what do ***I*** want or need, what's ***my*** role" to "what does this situation, or life itself require?" is a quintessentially Yin mature move.

One **Monster** impeding Yin spiritual maturity can be the belief that the Yang way is the right--and only--way. Cultures of secrecy and shame are often powerful inhibitors of spiritual growth, tricky because they can also present as spiritual support. When we experience depression, addiction, cynicism, apathy, over-individuation ("it must all be my fault") and the corresponding self-abnegation, we are wrestling with the monsters of spiritual maturity. And we must each find our own path past those monsters, perhaps (rarely) by slaying them, perhaps by befriending them, always by learning to sit with them.

---

[1] Kahlil Gibran, ***The Prophet***

Your Story

1. As you read about the Connection/Love aspect of Yin Spiritual Maturity, what comes up for you? Does this describe your own experiences of the spiritual? Do feeling gratitude and a desire to give back have a draw for you? What other aspects of the spiritual are important to you?

2. On the Autonomy/Curiosity side, how would you describe yourself? Do you find yourself drawn to being "in service," or is there still a pull to figuring out "what's ***my*** role?"

3. Which of the Monsters that inhibit/prevent spiritual maturity show up in your story? How? Are there others not mentioned? Give examples.

4. As you think about this form of maturity, what draws you to it? What repels you? How would you describe your relationship to it?

n Terry Tempest William's ***When Women Were Birds,*** she notes at the end;

> *I thought I was writing a book about voices. I thought I would proclaim as a woman that we must speak the truth of our lives at all costs. But what I realize...is that I will never be able to say what is in my heart, because words fail us, because it is in our nature to protect, because there are times when what is public and what is private must be discerned. There is comfort in keeping what is sacred inside us not as a secret, but as a prayer.*
>
> *The world is already split open, and it is in our destiny to heal it, each in our own way, each in our own time, with the gifts that are ours.*[1]

By now it should be clear that the boundaries of these four domains of maturity~physical, intellectual, emotional, spiritual~ are, like all Yin processes, intertwined, diffuse and subtle. Understanding these maturities in both their Yin and their Yang form represents a lifetime's work in growth (or more.) They ebb and flow like tides, depending on where we are in our lives. And there is no one Right Way to navigate those tides.

So how does this all come together? In circles and spirals, radiating rings in a pool of water. Becoming comfortable in one's own skin, full of fierce yet gentle curiosity and loving kindness, deeply faithful to human spirit, with an impulse of merciful concern that asks big questions and invites big answers. In the language of the Medicine Wheels, integration of Yin and Yang produces Flower Soldiers--women and men with the courage, discipline and heart to explore the directions both deeply and broadly. People who can be both fierce and gentle in service of what matters.

> *The Flower Soldier learns, with time and Self study, that Death is always present with Life. But Death is not the enemy. And Life is not the enemy. Life and Death are the great Teachers of Existence."*[2]

And it comes together in what Sharon Blackie describes as "Sovereignty." Sovereignty as autonomy, as our right to decide all aspects of our own lives, and to have that right respected with grace. As she notes, "the Heroine's Journey is also a quest for the Grail--but our path to it is a different route, for we *are* the Grail...the fertile, creative, life-giving energy of the universe...the energy we need to find within ourselves and bring out into an ailing world."[3]

---

11 Williams, op. cit., p. 228

2 Storm, op. cit., p. 339

3 Blackie, Sharon, ***If Women Rose Rooted***, p. 236

Your Story

1. Knowing that there is not "one right way," how do these forms of maturity come together for you, both now and in the person you aspire to be?

2. Is the concept of being a "Flower Soldier"--strong and soft, tender and tough--appealing to you? Is there another phrase to describe someone who is mature in all domains that you prefer?

3. What does the term "sovereignty" mean to you? Can you think of times when you've had sovereignty in your life? Describe.

4. When Sharon Blackie says, "we *are* the Grail…the fertile, creative, life-giving energy of the universe…the energy we need to find within ourselves and bring out into an ailing world," where does that land in your body? How does it relate to experiences you have had? Describe.

Chapter Eight: Defining Leadership

y favorite leadership definition remains this: "Leaders create worlds other people want to belong to."[1] Sixteen years ago I said this about leadership:

The stories told today about leadership -its nature, its impact, how it works and what is required of leaders-simply are not big enough for the times we live in. New levels of stewardship and responsibility, bigger-picture thinking and more encompassing hearts are needed by twenty-first century leaders. That will not happen without building a story about leadership that invites great wisdom and maturity, as well as a deep capacity for love and compassion. Leaders are needed whose hearts and minds are big enough for the job.[2]

In our divided world, and in the face of multiple global crises, it is fascinating to see that many of the leaders showing up with those big hearts and minds are women. According to CNN on 4/28/2020, only 10 of 152 elected heads of state were women.[3] Seven of them lead the countries that, by all measures, have had the most effective pandemic response.

Writing ***Speak the Truth and Point to Hope***, I got a lot of pushback for my ultimate conclusion: that love was at the core of truly mature leadership. In fact, I was told it was a dangerous thing to say. I responded:

Yes, it is dangerous ground. If we learned to

> *recognize that love was at the core of mature leadership, leadership that is generous and generative, forgiving and disciplined, leaders that create the worlds we secretly yearn for, we would indeed pose problems. Because we would not settle for the leadership we currently have. We would ask our leaders to ask* ***us*** *the hard questions. We would ask our leaders to invite us into the conversations where meaning gets made and value established. We would know that the famous leaders are rarely the great leaders. We would know that the way we recognize the mature leaders is through the way they make* ***us*** *feel and act: bigger, stronger, more generous, competent, capable and committed to our own highest values.*[4]

And that is still true. So how might mature leadership based in Yin, how might *we*, show up differently?

There are four important attributes present when leadership is mature in Yin as well as Yang: The first is that caring and concern become the central organizing principle of our decision-making processes. Putting human life--both in quantity and quality--as a, if not *the* factor around which policy is built reflects high maturity in all the directions. In the Medicine Wheels' belief system, for example, no law can pass through what is called "the Circle of Law" if it hurts the children.

A second attribute is insistence on and reinforcement of collaboration in our decision-making. Autocracy does not serve maturity;

indeed, it keeps both the autocrat and his or her followers stuck in immaturity. That does not bring out the best in anyone. Recent research indicates that an effective way to counter implicit bias is to ask for unanimity in decision-making. Anything less results in diverse voices being silenced.[5] That is the highest form of collaboration.

The third attribute is a commitment to grounded truthfulness, the ability to say what is known and acknowledge what is not known. To have a voice and not be afraid to use it. To ask different questions and propose different solutions. To reach this, we need to own our voices, our Yin knowing.

And the last attribute is generativity, being imaginative enough, creative enough to see where hope might lie. Not a false, Pollyana-ish hope, but true hope in the sense of being able to imagine a different, better world, and see one or two steps we could take to move in that direction. In other words, with full Yin, leaders do indeed ***speak the truth and point to hope***.

---

[1] Dilts, Robert, ***Visionary Leadership Skills: Creating a World to Which People Want to Belong***

[2] Marshall, ***Speak The Truth and Point to Hope, The Leader's Journey to Maturity***, p. 10

[3] www.cnn.com/2020/04/14/asia/women-government-leaders-coronavirus-hnk-intl/index.html

[4] Marshall, op. cit., p. XXIII

---

[5] ttps://magazine.byu.edu/article/when-women-dont-speak/?fbclid=IwAR1jdIUfzdHln3Or5GxDW7Wg8abXGUV9JErEkttDFih_JKLhiyCLrT9mu1M

Your Story

1. How does this description of Yin/Yang balanced leadership land for you? Does it describe someone you aspire to be, or someone you would be willing to follow? Describe your response.

2. Where, in your life, are you a leader? How comfortable are you in that role?

3. Which of the four elements of leadership grounded in Yin are you most comfortable with? Least? Do you know the sources of that comfort or discomfort?

4. Tell a story of a time when you spoke the truth and pointed to hope. What was that experience like for you?

Chapter Nine: Exploring the Yin Journey

et me be explicit: while I wrote this in part to explain how the Yin version of the Hero's Journey is different than the traditional, Yang journey, the Yin Journey is not just about or for women--it's for all who seek to find their voice and their balance, all who seek wholeness. All who are willing to step into their adult powers. All who find maturity a worthwhile goal.

The Hero's Journey architecture has a number of key elements--preparation, the call, accepting the call, embarking on the journey, encountering the monsters, discovering allies, achieving the goal, and returning home, the same and different. We will now explore each of these from a Yin perspective in more detail.

Preparation

ong before we know we are called to become adults, preparation for the Journey begins. It begins with your family of origin--were/are you allowed to be the person you are, or asked to be someone else? Was/Is your voice heard? Or is there pressure to act in specific ways--so that you are a person who reflects well on their family, a person who makes one or both parents feel good about themselves, a person without opinions or thoughts of her/his/their own? Is there a constant, covert or overt message that somehow you are not good enough, not measuring up, somehow disappointing?

What stories were you told? Were they stories of failure and redemption, stories of persevering and succeeding? Or were they stories of effortless accomplishment, where everyone was always successful? Did your family make everything glossy, or were the warty stories told as well? Were there events unexplained, histories hidden, people who disappeared and were never talked about again? All these tell us what is possible.

As humans, our childhood is our preparation. Parents, of course, often unconsciously reflect and re-enact their own childhoods, and the messages *they* were given. This is one reason trauma has such a tenacious hold on many families and communities. The hard work of breaking such a cycle requires great courage and discipline. Often it happens only if we find teachers, coaches, counselors or other adults who perceive us, and make us feel like they *know* we matter. These are people who can see in us the future mature being, and help to coax that being into the present.

The Call

he Yin Call is a felt sense, often of unbearable urgency, that life is asking you to do something. Like the urge to push in the process of childbirth, the Yin Call asks us to bring forth new life in many forms that sustain and nurture for the long term. "The Yin calling is to create home, not leave home. (The word economy comes from the Greek for 'creating home.'")[1]

The Yin Call is sourced in a profound yearning, a "true longing." That phrase comes from a David Whyte poem, "The Sea", wherein he describes

> *Our*
> *Wordless, fiery, unspoken,*
> *Hardly remembered,*
> *Gift of true longing."*[2]

As Whyte notes, "Longing comes from the body, ambition comes from the mind." Longing is Yin, ambition is Yang. We need both and have only one--ambition--these days. That longing, at its fundamental level, is to enact our impulse, need, desire for balance and wholeness. It can take the form of deciding not to work in a place or way in which we feel fundamentally unbalanced, or in a "wake-up" moment in which we realize our life is not the one we want, that something important is missing, as well as in all the traditional ways "calls" show up. And it is always about creating a home for ourselves, in the sense of creating a place where we can be whole.

The poet Alexis de Veaux notes, "Motherhood is not simply the organic process of giving birth. It is an understanding of the needs of the world."[3] In the same way, the Yin call is a deeply loving and instinctive working to speak, establish and enrich the connection that nurtures and cares for self and others, where the Yang Call may be more autonomy-oriented; proving our worth in the world, and contributing materially to our community .

Being the Hero (Shero?) in Your Own Story

ccepting the Call requires moving from a passive to an active role in our life. It is about relinquishing the Sleeping Beauty role and stepping up to waking ourselves up. It is learning to be receptive without relinquishing our autonomy. That means finding our balance between receiving protection and being the protector, between being the provider and being provided for, between all our active and passive voices/lives. Another way to speak of this is to say that we "self-authorize", we become the person who decides what our life is going to look, sound and feel like. We learn to follow our intuition, to trust our own ways of knowing.

In the end, accepting the Call is also about stepping up to face death in all its forms; the death of our own ego, our hopes and fears, the deaths of those we love, and the death we all ultimately undertake in the last chapter of our story. This has a great deal to do with our personal and cultural stories about maturity as well as dying. Do we seek elderhood or run from it? Accepting the Yin Call is ultimately accepting the call to maturity, to elderhood.

Monsters

s I've said before, trauma appears to be at the root of much of what keeps us crippled or paralyzed, unable to take ownership of our lives and our actions. And experiencing Yin moments can be extremely re-stimulating for those with a past history of trauma experiences. The dark, the silence, the seeming isolation, the inability to see a way ahead, that "dark night of the soul" kind of experience can be especially painful and frightening. We may not know with our conscious mind where our avoidance patterns come from if our trauma is rooted in preverbal experiences or experiences so terrifying that survival required dissociating from them. Trauma is a very real and very big Monster! The good news is that we finally have good tools for healing it.

Closely related to trauma can be insecure or failed attachment. This refers to ways in which our caregiver's (e.g. parent's) issues prevented them from truly seeing us as children and caused them to use us instead to satisfy or fulfill the unmet needs of *their* childhood. As Judith Blackstone notes, "Often children need to choose between the two sides of maturation: inward contact with themselves and connection with others."[4] When forcing that developmental choice is normalized by the dominant culture, then indeed, we take a risk by working to become whole and balanced, to have our Yin and Yang in healthy complementarity.

Both of those Monsters illuminate the deepest, biggest Monsters: the degree to which we have internalized the racism and misogyny of the last five thousand years. When we *believe* that we are "less than" in important ways, when we believe that Yin qualities--and our bodies--are dirty or disgusting, when we believe that what matters to us is fundamentally inferior to what matters to the Yang world, we have "drunk the Koolaid." We are poisoned in our thinking and feeling, and the struggle to rid ourselves of that poison in a fierce one indeed.

A smaller yet potent Monster for those on the Yin journey is our negative story about maturity. We may equate maturity with dullness, boringness and rule enforcement or aging and decrepitude, rather than a time when we can rest and regain our deepest joy. We don't embrace elderhood, perhaps because there is no social embrace of it. (Have you noticed? In modern culture, "mature" is often used as code language for pornographic, as is "adult.") There is no longer an equation of maturity with dignity and wisdom. It is no longer a state where we can expect to be appreciated and treated well. This is true for all of us, and an especial issue for women, whose value continues to be largely related to their attractiveness, rather than their contributions.

A final Monster is our failure to acknowledge that we can't exist without each other, that we are built to be in community. While once we celebrated "the common good," it has been replaced, as Robert Reich noted in his book, ***The Common Good,*** by a kind of "each man for his self, women and children be damned." One of the peculiar gifts of the pandemic of 2020 may be that whole segments of society are recognizing that we can't go it alone, that our sense of intrinsic self-worth is intimately bound up in our relationships with one another. As a species, we are not built to survive alone, even as our journeys are ours, individually.

In the Yang Journey, the Monsters are vanquished, slain, destroyed. In the Yin Journey, the monsters are greeted, acknowledged, walked along side of, and in many cases, befriended. In the dark, receptive warmth of Yin, Monsters reflect the "letting go and giving over" process that is required to acknowledge our traumas and our biases, accept our flaws, face our fears and move forward. As author Scilla Elworthy says, "Love is the only response to fear that works."[5] Yin invites us to love ourselves, because it acknowledges the darkness, allows parts of us to die and brings forth new growth..

The Journey -- Reaching for Maturity

aturity is that evolution of our fundamental drives for connection and autonomy into the capacity for love and curiosity. It happens, as I've said, in those four domains or directions, sometimes simultaneously, sometimes separately. But why DO we have to take a journey? Why should we mature? Biologically, the answer is simple: life evolves. It goes from simplicity to complexity. Humans are no exception. And only in and through maturity can we face and manage that complexity.

The Journey is the progression of our lives towards maturity, and ultimately to death, both of our egos and then our bodies. It is the path our lives take, usually only seen retrospectively as a series of journeys, a cycling through the four domains (aka the Four Directions). Each time, there is an experience of the Pit--the place where we meet our Monsters and walk with or through them.

So what does that mean here? The Journey asks that we step into the unknown and unknowable, and face our deepest fears. While that is equally true of the Yang journey, how we do the Yin Journey is very different. The Yin Journey is about interior movement, not achievement. It is the deep inner journey to find our interior spaciousness, to "compost," to rest quietly and at peace in the world, as the world is. It is a spiraling path, wherein we pass certain key points again and again, subtly or not so subtly different and more mature each time. It is on the Journey that our old self dies, enabling us come back with a new, more powerful voice to speak our truths into the world.

In the Medicine Wheel teachings, "Learning is a living challenge. It is the greatest and most holy of all human experiences. Discovery of the human Self is the highest of all knowledge."[6] When we only take the Yang Journey, the journey in the Light, we miss fully half of that holy experience, half of the discovery of our self. We do not discover that which is below the surface, in the dark, what is in our deep unconscious. That is where Yin takes us.

---

[1] Conversation with Laurie Marshall, artist and educator, 8/19 referring to Charles Eisenstein's book, ***Sacred Economics.***
[2] David Whyte, "The Sea," ***Where Many Rivers Meet***, pp.9-10
[3]https://www.ted.com/talks/yifat_susskind_in_uncertain_times_think_like_a_mother?language=en
[4] Blackstone, op. cit., p.12
[5] Elworthy, Scilla, ***Power and Sex, A Book About Women,*** p.130
[6] Storm, op. cit., p. 326

Your Story

1. Which elements of the Yin Journey resonate deeply for you? Do you know why? Elaborate....

2. Which elements do you recognize as underdeveloped in your current story? Do you know why? Explain....

3. What are the biggest monsters you have faced in your story so far? How have you conquered them? What are some of the ones still awaiting you? How might you address them?

4. Maturity can't be achieved without facing the inevitability of death – our loved ones' and our own. Describe your experiences with death to date. How do you relate those experiences to the idea of discovering "that which is below the surface, in the dark, in our deep unconscious?"

Chapter Ten: The Merry Many – Uniquely Yin Archetypes and Allies

In the great stories, the Heroes always have companions. This is true for leaders on a Yin journey too, though they often have a different set of allies. These allies come in archetypal forms, some functioning internally, some externally. If anything, Allies are even more important for the Yin Journey. It is the community that supports us.

Typically, the archetypes as they have been described are very Yang and/or male. I'm proposing a set of archetypes that instead specifically support Yin Journeys. They're organized in three phases to correspond to phases of our lives/journeys; archetypes of youth, archetypes of creatrix (the generative), and archetypes of maturity and balance. None of us have all these archetypes in our lives--or our selves--at all times, but when we're feeling especially lost or confused by where our Journey is taking us, it can be useful to ask "who do I need at this time?" and "who might fill that role for me?"

Archetypes of Youth – the Preparation Phase

These are the archetypes that can serve and support us in the first phases of our Yin Journey, the preparation phase, reflecting childhood and adolescence.

Shirley Temple: The Child

This archetype is often the purveyor of childish joy, playful, mischievous, full of curiosity, wanting to explore. Hyemeyohsts Storm notes, "Watch children on the playground--boys take ground, girls dance through."[1] It is the archetype of hope, celebrating life. Her struggles come when she is cast in the victim role or has to learn to sacrifice illusions without letting go of ideals.[2] Her role in your personal posse is probably as the eternal, delightful optimist.

Sleeping Beauty: The Virgin

This is the innocence archetype: trusting, naïve, pure, idealistic, pre-experience. She is passive, receptive to whatever life brings her, although she may also be transitioning to awareness of her own sexuality. She is often considered the most Yin archetype. The dark side of this archetype is the complete lack of responsibility for her life, for enacting her own wishes and desires. Conversely, her role is to remind you what the purest version of life could be.

Joan of Arc: The Martyr/Rebel

This archetype reflects the self-righteous determination of adolescence, in service of and strongly attached to some sort of ideal. It can be the archetype of the provider and protector or the destroyer, willing to lose everything for what she thinks is right. Its shadow is that it can be self-sacrificing to a fault for a false ideal, such as when it takes the form of anorexia or bulimia. Her role is to push you towards clarity about what really matters.

The Amazon

The Amazon archetype is fiercely protective of those she loves. She deliberately works to have physical and mental strength, constantly pushing herself to increase her capabilities. She is often but not always a "jock," and quite competitive. Like her male Warrior counterpart, at her best, she is deeply committed to service for the greater good. And she shares many of their shadow side issues – getting caught up in competition for competition's sake, valuing brute force over finesse, etc. Her role is to help you know that you are strong and can endure, as well as to create a strategy for succeeding.

Archetypes of Creatrix – the Midlife Phase

These are the archetypes of the Journey through midlife, representing roles we may assume or need around us as we make our way. Creatrix is the force for generativity, the energy that makes art, has babies, grows gardens, does innovative science, builds businesses, invents, counsels, heals and teaches.

The Healer

This is one of the oldest archetypes, often called the witch or the nurse. She learned to heal because she was herself wounded. She knows how to listen extraordinarily deeply, to people, plants and the planet. She recognizes that current scientific/medical wisdom is often flawed or limited and has the strength to go her own way, looking to plants and nature to support healing. Her shadow is that she may not have fully healed her own wounds, and can be tempted to use her knowledge against those she feels played a part in her wounding. Her role is to articulate, support and role model a healthy life.

The Mother/Daughter

This caregiver archetype is another ancient one, most often in the form of Hestia or Demeter.[3] She embodies nurturing and support. The Mother/Daughter understands that families are structures built in time and space, and that it is important to play the game for the long haul. Her shadow is the dreaded "smother mother" who emotionally eats her children. Her role is to support and reassure when things are at their darkest.

The Teacher

The Teacher archetype is driven to share her knowledge and skills. She has the gift of seeing through to the essential elements, breaking learning into its simplest parts and sharing those in ways that encourage and support her students' learning. She knows how to go slow at the beginning in order to go fast later on. Her shadow is the Yang intellectual pedant, fascinated by the sound of her own voice, and not in true service to learning. Her role is to encourage and explore next steps in the darkness.

Auntie Mame: The Wild Aunt

This strong feminine presence creates new roles and possibilities for us, with her adventurous, free-spirited, sexual and creative life. She can also be the feminine trickster. Her dark side is exemplified by Kali, the rageful Destroyer of evil forces in Hindu mythology. Her role is to be an ongoing invitation to explore and question assumptions--why DO things have to be a certain way?

Archetypes of Balance

"We shall not cease from exploration
And the end of all our exploring
Will be to arrive where we started
And know the place for the first time."[4]

These are the archetypes of maturity and elderhood, symbolizing "the Return," in Campbell's language. It is the time we bring our gifts in full flower to the community.

The Queen

The Queen is concerned for the well-being of all, including the least of her subjects. This is the archetype that holds sacred space for the feelings and the knowing of the collective unconscious. By recognizing and honoring them, she attends to the emotional and spiritual health of the whole kingdom. She embodies her story with full agency and authority, such that although her decisions may be discussed, they are rarely resisted. Her dark side is, of course, the Evil Empress who cares only for herself or her own family and exploits the rest of the kingdom. Her role is to illuminate, embody and role model the full power of feminine authority.

The Grandmother: the Archetypal Elder

Anthropologists note that in tribes with strong and healthy grandmothers, the whole tribe thrives. Without them they fail. The Grandmother holds the family or tribe together. She tells the family stories that give identity to the grandchildren or tribe and often is responsible for making sure key rituals are enacted.

Grandmother also tends the hearth, and feeds the children. She sits in the councils and quietly advises. Her dark side may show as preferring her own grandchildren and not treating all equally. Her role is to model "back-of-the-room" leadership that earns respect and does not require titles. Jungian analyst Marion Woodman notes, "She is alarmingly present. Like a tuning fork, her truth shatters hypocrisy. Others in her presence are released into what is true in themselves. Or flee."[5]

The Poet

The poet is the namer, the wise woman. Her role is to give us language for what we're experiencing. She has a self-possessed, solitary quality, even as she is part of the team, the village, the tribe. She keeps her own counsel unless asked, and is an exquisitely acute observer of human behavior as well as the natural world. She also knows her history. The poet traditionally was:

> *"…trained to step in at crucial times of difficulty and through extemporaneous speech bring sense and clarity to the confusion of the moment, and through that give the people some sense of their beckoning collective future. In a real sense, then, the poet brought together past, present and future in one utterance. [Her] responsibilities were great and [her] place in society honored."*[6]

Her shadow may be that, valuing her independence and solitude, she is reluctant to participate, at times when her voice is needed.

The Grower

The Grower feeds the community. Like the Healer, she knows the lunar cycles, where and when to plant, when to harvest, and when to lie fallow, and honors each season. She lives in balance and harmony with the natural world. She knows that humans have gardened since time immemorial, working with, not against, nature to enhance the viability of all. She is ruthless in her pruning and tender with her seedlings. Her dark side occurs when she becomes seduced by the power of genetics, and believes she can create and distort nature for her own ends. The Grower understands that gardens, like families, are structures in time and space. This allows her to be comfortable with timelessness--a bridge between the structures and the infinite. Her role is to teach about seasons, cycles, time and timing.

* * * *

These are far from being all the possible archetypes. They are ones, however, that can be especially helpful for those on the journey to find their voice. Yin times ask us to reach deeper into the archetypal field, what Jung called "the collective unconscious." In Christina Baldwin's classic ***Calling the Circle, the First and Future Culture***, she notes that Jung came to believe that the collective unconscious was where we all become one. He commented that the circle was a very ancient symbol, "one of the mythic motifs springing from the collective unconscious."[7]

Sharon Blackie writes that life and death are in a constant cycle. We simply can't have one without the other. Our modern way of seeing and being wants only the life part; we fear and despise the dying part. Blackie observes:

> *...death constantly gives birth to life. In order to embrace the creation of life, you must be able to live with the knowledge of death. This is the heart of what it is to be fully a human being. It is also the heart of our old native ways of knowing: the Celts view time, and so life, as cyclical rather than linear.*[8]

It's not surprising then, that Women's Circles often function as the prototype for organizing one's allies on the Yin Journey...and that the circle itself becomes the Journey archetype. Over and over, women's stories reflect this circling quality. For Baldwin, circle is the symbol of community:

> *Community is universal reality. From the atomic level on up, community is the pattern set into the design of the world....Invisible circles of atoms cluster into molecules, combining in marvelous diversity to create all that is. Things group together by attraction and affinity....We live on a planet where creatures move in herds, flocks, packs, prides, families and tribes. We thrive best in the company of others....Community is our social-genetic inheritance.*[9]

Community, is, for many of us in the 21st century, however, a double-edged sword: we yearn to be perceived and are terrified of it, we want to belong yet maintain our independence, on and on. We have outsourced and commodified many of the functions community once served. Ultimately, community is where we play out all the battles of our needs for autonomy and connection, our addiction to Yang and our desperate need for Yin. Baldwin notes:

> *The shadow in the circle is an opportunity to practice*
> *compassion for what is unhealed in all of us - and at*
> *the same time to practice fierceness in protecting*
> *the delicate interpersonal bonds of community.*[10]

---

[1] Author conversation with H. Storm, 10/15

[2] Pearson, Carol, ***Awakening the Heroes Within***, p. 80

[3] Hestia was the Greek goddess of the hearth, Demeter, goddess of the harvest, sacred law, and the cycle of life and death. Persephone, her daughter, was kidnapped and taken to the underworld, thus creating the story of winter and summer.

[4] Eliot T.S., ***Four Quartets, Little Gidding, II***

[5] Woodman, Marion, ***Leaving My Father's House; A Journey to Conscious Femininity***, p. 202

[6] Whyte, David, ***The Heart Aroused: Poetry and the Preservation of the Soul in Corporate America***, p. 164

[7] Baldwin, Cristina, ***Calling the Circle,*** p. 28

[8] Blackie, op. cit., p. 351

[9] Baldwin, op. cit., p. 192

[10] Ibid. p. 174

Your Story

1. As you think about these archetypes, which ones have the deepest resonance for you? Tell stories from your life that illustrate why and how they are important.

2. Which archetypes would be useful to call into your life at this time, and for what reason?

3. What communities are you a part of? Tell a story about a time your community supported you....or failed to.

4. How has the shadow shown up in a community you've been part of? What did you learn from it?

Chapter Eleven: The Return

n Campbell's construct, the Return is the bringing of our gifts back to our community. It also is the closing of one cycle, and the opening of another. In Yin times, the return is a return to what matters, to what is fundamental: Fundamental to our identities, fundamental to our health, fundamental to our hearts and spirits. In the Yin journey, the Return does not focus on public recognition for the gifts we bring, it focuses on the internal recognition, what we now know about ourselves. It focuses on the greater balancing of Yin and Yang energies we have achieved. It is demonstrated by speaking our truths.

Historically, the Return has often been framed as having recovered something, e.g., brought back the Holy Grail. For some scholars, the Grail represents the integration of the Yin with the Yang, given that it is a cup, a symbol of the receptive. For me, the Grail symbolizes the ability to fill ourselves with our voice, our sovereignty, our power and our right to make the choices that affect us.

Elderhood: Where Journeys End

The Medicine Wheels teach that:

> *It takes a Lifetime to know the self....We are alive, here with wondrous Mother Earth, to get to know our Self. It is the fact of our Life that will give us Measure and teach us of the Essence of who we are. This is the primary reason for our existence.*[1]

Interestingly, in indigenous cultures, elderhood status is accorded to those who have "the ability to see the world from someone else's point of view, without fearing the loss of one's own position."[2]

> *"Confronted with the task of discovering a path to reconciliation and cooperation in a time of unprecedented threat to human existence, elders focus on the idea that the primary organizing principle for human achievement is stability, not progress, meaning that balance, symmetry and regularity are more to be valued than change, growth, deviation and ambition."*[3]

"But, but, wait! NO change? Isn't that a terrible idea?" That's not what's been said here. Elders understand that change comes, as do seasons. Their designing of right relationships, however, focuses on that which can be a source of stability to humans, such as family and community, rather than the next bright shiny object. Change for change's sake, change to speed things up, change to keep us constantly entertained without ever knowing how to be fully present on our beautiful planet -- those things are not valued by elders.

Elderhood is the place where we own our archetypes and our ancestors. As writer, teacher and story-teller Stephen Jenkinson says, "the elder is a visitation of the Old Ones, one's ancestors."[4] If we have done our work, it is the place where we set down and set free our traumas and those of our Ancestors. The place where we remember or design and then tell the stories that will sustain our children.

Healthy elderhood is an invitation to lay down competition and the fight for recognition. It is where, if we haven't already, we can relinquish *power over* for *power with*. It is where domination is fully replaced by cooperation. [5] Where our power comes from our balance, which is actually the ability to re-balance quickly rather than a permanent state. It is the time to ask, "what best serves the common good?" and build the alliances, networks and communities that make that common good work. Elders who do this "become the keepers of the teachings and rituals that allow the tribe to flourish, and...uphold the social order."[6] Such elderhood is where our power lies in a full and rich understanding of our worth, our impact, our resources and our gifts. It is where Yin and Yang meet in full complementarity.

Unfortunately, in U.S. culture, healthy elderhood is a concept without a visible constituency. Indeed, we seem allergic to the idea. It certainly is *not* driving a huge RV down the road with a bumper sticker proudly proclaiming "I'm spending my children's inheritance." Nor is it investment in face-lifts and private trainers so that we can delude ourselves into thinking that aging can be hidden, and we can stay "forever young." Yet, in a world where to be old is to be invisible, we can hardly blame those who are terrified by the prospect of such obliteration.

In First Peoples' cultures, elders are revered, not scorned. In Western culture, where technical fluency has replaced all other kinds of knowledge and passes for wisdom, it is the children who now teach their grandparents. Unaware that technical skills have an extremely short shelf-life, they can easily slide into smug assumptions about whose knowledge has real value. By the time young people today recognize that interpersonal skills and self-awareness are likely to matter far more in their lives than their technology prowess, often their grandparents are gone, along with the opportunity to understand their family history and learn from those stories.

In full elderhood, we know ourselves. Our maturities converge. We reach full balance--Yin *and* Yang, autonomy *and* connection, love *and* curiosity, physically, emotionally, intellectually, spiritually. We learn to negotiate the limits of our health, and no longer attempt to vanquish those limits.[7] Biologically, we all, however gendered, may lose the hormonal edginess that dominated us in our younger years. We become more alike than we had been. And, we know ourselves--in all directions. We know our place in the world and we belong to it.

Ultimately, elderhood brings us a kind of confluence, a maturity that unites Yin and Yang and listens exquisitely--to the self, to other people and to the rest of the beings that reside on Planet Earth. It acknowledges the great sorrows of our times, and the great joy of being alive. It brings us back to where we began as a species--with a full sense of our being and place in the cosmos. At home. At peace.

Can we imagine such a place?

---

[1] Storm, op. cit., p. 402

---

[2] Lopez, Barry, ***Horizon,*** p. 413.
[3] Ibid, p. 414
[4] Jenkinson, Stephen, ***Come of Age***, p. 193
[5] Ellworthy, op. cit., p. 80
[6] Blackie, op. cit., p. 343
[7] Jenkinson, op. cit., p. 192

Your Story

1.) The Return is where your story both begins and ends. It begins because this is the part you get to intentionally design. It ends because, well, all stories end. And then they begin again. What kind of elder do you want to be? Think carefully about the traits and qualities you would like to be known for at the end of your life and write them down.

2. What might you start to do now to ensure that you feel like there's a place in the world to which you belong? What practices could you develop that help ground in that place?

3. How mindful are you of how you treat the elders you know? Is it the way you would like to be treated at that stage of life? How could you deepen your appreciation of what elders have to offer?

4. After you read the section that follows, consider writing your own "Future Perfect." Not just how you want your life to be, but also what kind of world is required to make that possible? There are as many possibilities are there are stars.......which ones call to you?

Chapter Twelve: Future Perfect – Coming Full Circle: How It Could Be in a Balanced World

Just sing. Be on the side of the makers and shapers, the singers and the storytellers. That's all you need to do. Not to sing with the voice of an angel, but however cracked and broken your instrument, sing anyway.[1]

Future perfect, grammatical definition: *actions that have not yet occurred but will occur and be finished in the* ***future****.*

o create a different world, we must imagine a different world. I started thinking about this, how it could be, in my early 20's–50 some years ago. I'd read Ernest Callenbach's ***Ecotopia*** and found myself deeply moved. My dad assured me that a steady-state, no-growth economy was a terrible idea. "I'm not so sure you're right, Pop," I thought to myself. Now I know he wasn't.

The journey to a world in which Yin and Yang are in balance will be neither speedy nor easy. To create such a world, we have to begin by imagining all the ways this world might be different. As I've felt my way into understanding what is required to bring us into balance through understanding the Yin aspects of the leadership journey, "Future Perfect" seems to me a great phrase for what I want to do here: challenge us to design a far more beautiful world than the one we've been calling "normal." To be clear, this isn't a roadmap~that would be premature. "If you don't know where you're going, all roads will get you there." We need first to decide where we're going.

ere, with gratitude to Ernest Callenbach, Starhawk, Octavia Butler, Eric Holthaus, Charles Eistenstein, Jeannie Zandi, adrienne maree brown, Hyemeyohsts Storm and many other thinkers, is such a vision. A world of possibilities I invite you to explore. See what fits and what doesn't......and then consider what your contribution to birthing your "new normal" might be.

In my version, we'll focus on how a Yin-Yang balanced world could and would be different, including

- New language (in many languages) for bringing the challenging skills of the messy process of community building into every day parlance;
- Ways that families, whatever their form, can support all ages and help set strong emotional foundations;
- Approaches to the beginning and end of life not based in the constructs of fear and control, but instead reflecting an understanding that we begin and end in Yin;
- Spiritual lives imbued with vibrancy, gratitude and compassion that honor Creator and Creatrix, the web of Life;
- Lifestyles that invisibly embed healthy practices such that overall health and well-being increase dramatically;

- Rich educational practices that account for a full range of learning styles and encourage cooperation as well as healthy competition;
- An economy that focuses on generosity rather than accumulation, and ensures the fundamental well-being of all;
- A redistribution of population density as well as cultural vitality;
- An understanding of the role the arts play in the quality of our lives;
- Every human self-aware enough to know when they are "othering" and when they are building skills for inclusion, cooperation and unanimity;
- Leaders exalted for caring, having questions and listening and then building cooperative solutions;
- Citizens around the world enjoying regular, consistent community conversations about the things that matter to that community;
- Elders teaching of continually arising ecosystems and modeling the patience to understand and work with them.

So, friend, walk with me into the future and imagine these possibilities....

New Patterns of Language and Action

Getting to a Yin-Yang balanced world required a vast amount of shutting up and listening. The lesson that "taking it slow" is almost always the faster route took, unsurprisingly, time to fully integrate into people's bodies and behaviors. Local councils were formed everywhere as the primary decision-making tool. Taking time to discuss and explore at the front end, to insist on unanimity, to make sure that everyone's voice was heard, meant that when decisions *were* made (finally!) they could be executed rapidly and easily. There was no hidden resistance, no sabotage and subterfuge, everyone understood the why and the how and things moved forward with grace.

It was a painful adjustment, especially for those used to giving orders and having them carried out, or those used to following orders unthinkingly. Yet the order-givers ultimately recognized that having orders carried out "to the letter of the law" often resulted in "malicious compliance," wherein the "spirit of the law" was completely undone by cruel attention to (amounting to deliberate misinterpretation of) the details. They saw that almost any effort could be undone if there was not true unanimity as to why and how it was being done. And the order takers realized that, as citizens in a democratic nation-state, they could not evade the responsibilities of having thought through their decisions.

One way this has been enacted is to ask, in the Councils, "Who speaks for Wolf?[2]" The question comes from an old Native

American (Oneida) teaching story, a story rooted in the assumption that all forms of life have equal value--humans, plants and animals. The story told of a tribe that chose to move into an area inhabited by wolves, even though they were warned "I think you will find that it is too small a place for both [you and Wolf], and that it will require more work then--than change would presently require."[3] Predictably, the tribe was forced to move in the middle of winter, because it was indeed too small a place for both, and it was indeed more much work than had they changed when warned. As author Paula Underwood told the story,

AND SO IT WAS
That the people devised among themselves
A way of asking each other questions
Whenever a decision was to be made
On a New Place or a New Way
We sought to perceive the flow of energy
Through each new possibility
And how much was enough
And how much was too much
UNTIL AT LAST
Someone would rise
And ask the old, old question
To remind of us of things
We do not yet see clearly enough to remember
TELL ME NOW MY BROTHERS
TELL ME NOW MY SISTERS
WHO SPEAKS FOR WOLF?[4]

Who speaks for the forces that are neither friend nor enemy, but whose interests we impact? Without that voice, no good decisions can be made.

A closely related lesson had to do with technology adoption. Rather than unquestioningly embracing new technologies and tools as they came into being, people have learned to ask questions before adoption, as Amish communities have always done: "Is this good for the community?" "Does this contribute to our quality of life?" "Is it too fast or too much?" "How many or much of this technology do we need?" "How much is enough?" "How much is too much?"

Interestingly, these questions and linguistic patterns have led to new cultures in which requests and agreements are very carefully attended to and negotiated, and consent is well understood. People understand that "No" and "Yes" are both promises, and must be carefully considered. Knowing that requests are how both relationships and work begin, adolescents are taught by their elders to carefully make and think through their requests, to ask questions to make sure what they want is clear, and to only make agreements predicated on that clarity. In these cultures, listening skills and framing good questions are amongst the most highly rated skills a citizen can have.

The ability to hear what someone is saying, and then to hear beneath the words, to what those words actually mean and how they move the conversation forward, regardless of whether or not one agrees with them, is what earns one "elderhood" status (for people of any age). And it is the elders who are chosen for (elected to) key decision-making positions. People know elders can be trusted with the community's best interests, that their decisions will always benefit the children in the long run, and will never leave anyone behind.

Families

amilies are people who choose to live together, and often to raise children. They are multi-generational and often include people who are not biologically related, living in groups as small as five and as large as twenty. (They are one of the few things that get larger in a well-balanced Yin-Yang world! Not because there are more children, but because all people are welcomed.) Almost every family includes at least one elder, and some have as many as four. The elders frequently provide the social glue, the quiet attending to the needs of the children and the logistics of living with others--meals and maintenance. Children spend their first five years in a cohort of 3-6 peers, a bond that frequently lasts a lifetime, based on the old Okinawan system of life-time clans, called "moai".

Identities remain quite fluid in families. There is no assumption that the Yin or Yang domains belong to any gender. Children are invited to explore and choose, as a part of the coming-of-age process, where they see themselves on the gender spectrum. More precisely, every one, gendered or not, can take their turn in Yin or Yang--provider, nurturer, leader, partner--and does so with grace and composure, as the situation demands and their capabilities allow. Children do not grow up associating certain behaviors with a given parent's gender; they experience being invited to develop and adapt to responsibilities as befits their abilities.

Living embedded in such a dynamic family life gives both children and elders a vibrant, lively existence and the opportunity to feel--and be--valued. The richness of elders' stories transmits the values of harmony, symmetry and regularity and their behavior models balance and a deep inclusiveness, in which the concerns of all must be weighed before decisions are made. They have listening hearts, and with those hearts, they expand the courage and confidence of all they come into contact with.

Beginning and End of Life

omen's power to nurture life and give birth is deeply respected as a rich part of the nature of Yin-Yang balanced culture, whether or not they actually give birth. Birthing itself has returned to homes for the most part, unless there is a particularly high-risk pregnancy; then it is supported by skilled healers in well-equipped healing facilities. Midwifery is a respected life-choice, and midwives see to the wide range of health questions posed by the female body. Women make the decisions about whom the father of their children will be and men recognize it for the honor that it is; they share parenting responsibilities equally. There are rarely more than three children, and those are usually spaced at least four years apart, in order to keep birth rates low.

Like birth, dying as a part of the natural life cycle is well understood in nature-based societies such as these nation-states have become. The desperate clinging to life-extension that is the hallmark of cultures where no one ever fully lives has faded away. Death is accepted as part of the natural order of things, a final returning of our gifts to Mother Earth, which has fed and supported us our whole lives long. Many communities have developed beautiful processes for easing the dying person and her or his family through the final Return, with the help of the Healers if needed. What remains after Spirit departs is always offered to the land or sea, as food for the next cycle. People are unafraid to be present with the dying, and come to say their goodbyes, make their peace and offer or accept forgiveness if it is needed. Celebrations of the lives of loved ones who have Returned are rich, full of stories, laughter and tears.

Spiritual Life

There is an aliveness to people's sense of their spiritual life that is quite striking. Having been taught meditation, martial arts and grounding skills since childhood, along with a full panoply of wilderness survival skills, there is a deep sense of safety in the world running through their lives. It is easy to be "at home" in the world, and sense the underlying current and power of love, the humming vibrational field that animates us all.

Many of the old faiths are still practiced in various forms and combinations, although there is no intervention into the realms of governance or nation state boundaries as there once was. Temples, mosques, monasteries, abbeys and convents still exist for people whose being wants that focus, either for a time or a lifetime. Spiritual teachers are often based in such places, but may travel widely. The concept of the "frequency holder",[5] the grounded elder who makes the situation better simply by being there, is well understood, and often employed when passions are running high on a given issue.

Health and Wellbeing

In a world with far more physical activity and far fewer professions with deadlines, as well as unpolluted air and water, general health levels have unsurprisingly increased dramatically. Cancer rates and cardiac events have plummeted. Nutrition is widely understood as the first line of defense against disease of all kinds. Advanced medicine, as it was known in the West, exists in only a few nation-states, as the demand for it has declined. These resources are available free to those who need them, and there is a well-developed world-wide referral system to ensure that people get the help they need. Often, several nation-states will join together to create and fund a research institute to work on health challenges unique to a given area (such as sickle cell anemia or specific diseases).

While many communities have specific culinary histories and traits, there is widespread understanding that vegetables, fruits, spices, a variety of grains and wild or grain-free meats, as well as plant oils can be used in an almost infinite number of ways to create healthy, tasty and nutritious cuisines. Many nation states have culinary arts schools (always attached to a food forest or a farm) of which they are justly proud. Extensive exchange programs foster friendly national rivalries.

Starting at age five, all young people are taught basic centering and meditation techniques. In the inevitable conflicts of everyday life, there is almost always an elder nearby to help them recognize and name their feelings, and then to "use their words" to work out issues, whether with their peers or older folk. Additionally, no one becomes a parent without "Life" classes, taught by other, older parents that give them tools for coping with the challenges that parenting inevitably encounters. The parents in these classes bond deeply and frequently join in many child-rearing activities together.

That human beings are sexual creatures, and that sexuality can take a vast array of forms is well understood. From a young age, children are taught that their bodies are their own, and that touching or being touched by others without consent is inappropriate. Healthy intimate partner relationships in various configurations are well-modeled. Marriage is optional, and there are well-understood processes for ending partnerships/marriages, which are focused heavily on the well-being of the children (including the preservation of their moai). With so much less emphasis on acquiring property, relationship dissolution is far less emotionally fraught.

Education

he underlying premises of education have shifted from a heavy Yang emphasis on accomplishment and scores, to include equally Yin's emphasis on process depth, emotional intelligence and self-awareness. Children are consistently encouraged to express their feelings and then taught how to manage them, for their own wellbeing and that of their community. Emotional intelligence is as highly regarded and developed as other forms of intelligence, and is not considered the special province of females.

From infancy to age five, children are closely connected to their primary care givers and their resident elders. The caregivers in turn are given support and respite by the grandparents or resident elders. All children experience welcome and security in those first years, with strong attachments to those around them, and to their wise elders who are well-versed in healthy child development.

Between the ages of five and twelve, children spend most of their time out of doors, regardless of weather conditions. Education is project- and interest-based, with kids encouraged to study the natural world by teachers who are passionate about it, to build structures based on the homes of a wide variety of animals, insects and birds, and to develop a thorough understanding of their ecosystem. Learning to read, write and draw well are natural parts of this process, as well as the practical mathematics and other skills required for building.

Between twelve and twenty, there is a mix of longer, bigger projects and wilderness time. All children at thirteen undergo month-long Outward Bound[6] style experiences, drawing on the wilderness survival skills they have been learning since five. For those who want it, the onset of menses is celebrated with a month-long "away time" under the guidance of a council of mothers and women elders. These recognize that the female identity offers a different path to maturity than the male or those in-between. Those young people who identify as women learn to consistently align their activities with the lunar cycle, such that waxing is a time for full striving and waning is a time for rest and renewal. These patterns are understood and accepted, as it clearly enhances overall productivity, creativity and contribution.

For those who choose it, the "celebration of manhood," comes later, somewhere between 17 and 19, and is held, again, under the guidance of a council of fathers and male elders. Leading up to it are a series of increasingly stringent challenges, each customized for the young man-to-be that enable him to experience being in right relation to the Earth and all its beings. This almost inevitably includes physically and mentally testing oneself against a variety of significant (and often dangerous) obstacles, and is available to all who seek it. Some of the challenges are gender-specific, some specifically for LGTBQ or non-binary teenagers, some are local, some involve traveling to other countries and cultures.

For those young people whose sexual identity falls somewhere else, there is a clear and thoughtful process for choosing or not choosing a gender or sexual identity. No one is forced to be something they feel they are not. And, over the years, a variety of wonderful coming-of-age processes have been designed for such young people. In every case, the goal is to bring that young person to maturity with dignity and love. In all cases, there is a point at which each young person choses a name for themselves, based on the learning, experiences, or vision they have had. As Judith Pintar wrote in ***A Voice From the Earth***:

> *"Traditionally, this ritual made sure that all adolescents entered adulthood with some vision or purpose for which they were responsible. This was practical psychology, helping to ease the transition period for the young from the dependence of childhood to the responsibility of adult life.* [7]

Young people can pursue their passions and interests in a wide variety of domains, mentored by others with the same passions. They are expected to complete at least two significant, self-designed community service projects between eighteen and twenty. These may range from road and bridge building to a year on a farm to working as an EMT or fire-fighter. Entrepreneurship is widely encouraged, and many young people have flourishing small businesses by the time of their Coming of Age ceremony during their 20th year.

As has always been true, there are senior teachers in many fields, and young people may elect to apprentice themselves to one or a series of them, to further expand their learning and their skills. As examples; senior painters or sculptors, senior furniture, footwear or clothing makers, senior researchers of the past or the future, senior builders of homes, roads, bridges and footpaths, senior musicians and song-writers in a vast range of instruments and modalities, senior athletes and practitioners of the martial arts, senior explorers of land and sea, senior chefs, senior healers and herbalists or senior poets and storytellers. In all cases, they are known as much for their lack of self-aggrandizement as for their ability to open possibilities for those who work with them.

Economy

ndigenous activist and writer Lyla June Johnston notes that "economy and ecology are the same thing."[8] All these changes have become easier to enact as the economy slowed, and the environment healed. "Growth" is no longer the economy's primary focus, replaced instead by the idea of "fair and healthy exchange" and human dignity at every level. During the transition, governments instituted a basic income for all citizens, although, in many places, it was quickly superseded by an upwelling of entrepreneurial spirit --citizens seeing needs locally and moving to fill them. Still, the base income has remained, to support those having a health crisis, wishing to start a new enterprise, needing to survive a setback or wanting to pursue a project.[9]

People's attachment to "stuff" as the primary driver of identity has waned as alternate forms of self-expression have become more accessible--through hand-crafted clothing, for example. The emphasis on fashion as a driver of feminine identity has declined as the need for a distinctly feminine identity declined. People wear what suits their personalities, not what an "industry" has declared appropriate. And with the shriveling of "big" in business and industry, the subtle pressures for a specific kind of dress, a uniform signaling that you're part of the group, have lessened considerably.

Similarly, when people's homes are no longer a primary opportunity to flaunt one's wealth, but simply a place to live and nurture wellbeing for oneself and others, housing sizes have shrunk back to much older levels. Privacy no longer matters as much as community and connection. Where once generosity was expressed through philanthropy (and generally got you a building named after you, or at least an endowed chair at a university), more and more generosity is expressed through the ancient form of the "give-away." This is a recognition that, through hard work and good luck, you have amassed more than you need, and, in ceremony, you have elected to redistribute that wealth within your community. Thus, one person's good fortune becomes the community's good fortune, and material goods no longer accrete, but keep circulating in the community. Great honor and respect is accorded someone who "gives away."

The issues of 20th century capitalism--debt (including personal, corporate and national), trade imbalances, exploitation of labor and resources in poor countries, and the continuing accumulation of wealth by a few--have diminished dramatically as every region has taken self-sufficiency as its first goal. It has been fascinating to watch the ways refugee camps, full of the victims of climate change and the resulting wars, become nation-states in their own right, evolving systems of governance and teaching their inhabitants to raise their own food and access water, even in the desert regions. In many cases, young service workers from nearby countries have played a major role in this transformation.

To get here, a century and half of laws that gave corporate entities the same rights as citizens has been unraveled and replaced by laws that made clear the primacy of the rights of children to a healthy future and the rights of the natural world to exist unexploited and unpolluted. Those who violated these new laws were, for a time, heavily criminalized and punished.

More importantly, no new projects of any kind, no new "development," can be initiated until a thorough analysis of its upstream and downstream implications has been completed, using a variation on the "Circle of Law" process (described under Governance section). "Upstream" means figuring out if the problem the project was designed to solve could be better handled prior to the project's point of intervention. [10] "Downstream" means an accounting for *all* project costs--resources, wastes, and impact on earth, water and sky. "Cradle to cradle"[11] has become the mantra, meaning that anything built has to be made of natural materials which can be returned to the soil for composting or otherwise returned to the ecosystem at the end of its life.

The move to permaculture[12] as the primary form of agriculture has dramatically altered the food landscape and solved the problems of the food supply chain. People have recognized that "convenience" is a poor trade for nutrition, and that seasonality actually improves the quality of their menus, even if they don't get to have "everything, all the time." This form of agriculture has dramatically altered the physical landscape as well. Hundreds of thousands of acres of parking lots and highways have been torn up and replanted as food forests. The blacktopped wastelands surrounding most urban areas have become food-producing communities, water has returned (or been uncovered) and villages have grown up in these formerly barren areas. The complex food distribution systems of the 20th and early 21st century have been replaced by local access for the bulk of one's food.

With these moves has come a drastic reduction in CO^2 emissions, meaning that climate change slowed, and then stopped. It took a few decades, but the Earth's amazing powers of regeneration have eventually turned the tide, and the desertification of much of the planet has subsided. With that, and the return to local control in most of the world, the vast immigrant tides of the late 20th and early 21st century have also diminished substantially. When they do happen, immigrants are welcomed, and there are clear protocols for integrating them into communities.

Most of the nation-states require at least two years of community service from their young people, some asking three, and in a few cases, four. (This depends on whether the service is also a form of apprenticeship.) Service is generally considered the next step after the Coming of Age Ceremony at twenty for young people. There are multiple options, or tracks that someone can choose, such as peace-keeper, agriculturalist, emergency medical technician, healing worker or forestry/bamboo manager. Each includes six to nine months of intensive training followed by eighteen to thirty-six months of service. "Careers" are no longer a focus. Now it is finding your calling and performing work you love.

All tracks are open to everyone. Young people who had already started businesses can apply to have their enterprise registered as a community enterprise if their passion is sufficient and they can prove community benefit (e.g., provides a community service, creates job opportunities, or community cultural enrichment.) Additionally, numerous nation-states have exchanges with neighboring states, increasing young people's language and culture skills, while helping to strengthen relations between the states. No one is excused from service.

Currencies

s global capitalism shrank, the hegemony of the American dollar did as well. Indeed, money's role in facilitating life shrank. Bartering arrangements became much more frequent. People's "needs" also shrank, as they grew to trust that their community would care for them, and they had the time and space to be creative in a vast number of ways. Slowly, local currencies evolved, because it is easier to use a trust-based currency when you know your neighbors, your local shops and services. Typically, every village had a currency, which was exchangeable with neighboring communities, and in some case, the same currency was used throughout an entire country.

Regional councils also could be convened to set exchange rates in the rare event that a large-scale project was being considered. Taxes, used to support local infrastructure such as roads, parks and meeting areas as well as recycling trash and transportation services were paid in these local currencies.

Cities

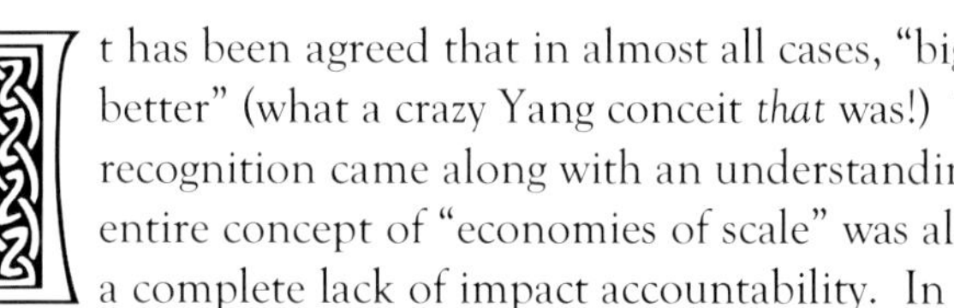

It has been agreed that in almost all cases, "bigger is NOT better" (what a crazy Yang conceit *that* was!) This recognition came along with an understanding that the entire concept of "economies of scale" was also rooted in a complete lack of impact accountability. In other words, the upstream and downstream impacts of an enterprise or institution were never factored into the balance sheets of said entity. Once society instituted mechanisms for recognizing precisely how large scale operations affect bio-systems' carrying capacity and the economy, a "small is beautiful" mindset took hold firmly. Older, less intrusive technologies were in some cases resurrected. In other cases, elegant new solutions were created for the ways that communities depend on one another.

City sizes shrank rapidly during the transition period, as the needs for things like "office space" and "retail space" dissolved. Some buildings were turned into living spaces, some removed to allow Mother Earth to breathe again. Much of the vibrancy associated with city living was redistributed, although a few of the oldest cities, following the Rule of 200 (the understanding that more than 200 humans in a location or enterprise was a recipe for long-term disaster because people would not know each other)[13], set a cap on population density in any given area. Cities now resemble clusters of villages, creating a far stronger sense of "neighborhood" and community. These are woven together through a variety of public transit options, along with parks and trails carefully thought out to create both "away" spaces and larger community gathering places in amphitheaters of various sizes.

Many of the attractions of cities--cafés, galleries, museums, music venues--are to be found in the villages, each of which has some kind of central square where people can gather to visit, eat and make music. And, of course, some villages have a particular claim to fame, such as a Culinary Arts school, an Art Institute, a research institute, a music school, a furniture making school or some other advanced craft school that draws people to a particular region. Again, the Rule of 200 helps prevent overpopulation of any given area, and the transit system makes it easy to live elsewhere and still take advantage of such resources.

The natural human impulse to congregate with one's "own," which historically was based on some sort of (believed) ethnicity as well as geographic proximity, while not completely gone, has been considerably refined. One's "tribe" has come to mean shared interests and ways of being as much as shared ancestry. This has intensified as the recognition that we all stand on the shoulders of our ancestors has increased. There are widely shared days of ancestor recognition and appreciation. While done very differently in different parts of the world, this common sense of being part of a great chain helps ground people and relieves some of the fear of death that was formerly so common.

The Arts

he arts are no longer the province of a specialized few. In a Yin-Yang balanced world, self-expression has become intrinsic to daily life, whether it's the patterns you paint on your house or the music you make or the worlds you write or the ways you share your skills with others. Ursula Le Guin put it this way;

> *Prose and poetry–all art, music, dance–rise from and move with the profound rhythms of our body, our being, and the body and beings of the world. Physicists read the universe as a great range of vibrations, or rhythms. Art follows and expresses those rhythms. Once we get the beat, the right beat, our ideas and our words dance to it, the round dance that everybody can join. And then I am thou, and the barriers are down.*[14]

In this world, the arts heal, the arts liberate, and the arts inform the community of what matters most. They amplify the rhythms of our living, breathing planet. Artists of all kinds are valued and respected.

Power Generation

key piece of the transformation to a balanced Yin-Yang world has been changing the way electrical power is generated and distributed worldwide. The giant towers marching across the landscape that were such a feature of the late 20th and early 21st century in westernized countries are gone. Power generation is a local phenomenon--locally created, distributed and managed. Every community has its own mix of solar, hydro, tidal and wind-generated power, depending on its location. People grow up acutely conscious of how much power an activity costs, and that is factored into their daily life planning.

The Boards responsible for managing power distribution are typically a mix of elected citizens, elders and members of their Councils who are well educated in this domain, Yin and Yang in equal number. In the event of a crisis, facilities such as wellness centers have sufficient backup to hold them for some time, as power storage is one technical area in which considerable resources have been invested. Because patent law has been stripped back to its original seven-year limitation,[15] ingenuity in this domain is rewarded but not excessively.

In nation-states where power generation is the most difficult, treaties with neighbors help to ameliorate imbalances so that no one suffers. Exchanges might include foodstuffs, tools, technology or manufacturing capabilities, all carefully worked out to keep power evenly distributed in every sense of the term. It helps that every treaty will have to pass through the Circle of Law (see Governance, below), because it removes temptations to unbalance the system.

Racism Faced

ver the years, people have learned some hard lessons. Hardest has been dispelling the myth of racial "color blindness," and then doing the hard work of seeing how deeply embedded racism and colorism were across the globe, economically, politically and socially. The work of recognizing and rooting out the vast array of prejudices humans hold towards one another, those deeply painful internal conversations about inferiority and superiority, were critical to dismantling Yang control and bringing Yin back into balance. And critical to rebuilding and reinforcing our thirst for justice, truth and reconciliation.

Naming power dynamics and developing the recognition of how they worked required new skill sets and new forms of self-awareness. The willingness to finally have those painful conversations laid the groundwork for societies whose maturity and courage have visibly increased. New forms of language--in many languages--with which to speak about and forgive one another's transgressions have developed. And our healing support for those who have been injured by these ugly "isms" has gotten much more realistic and effective.

In many places, this was accomplished through a variety of "restorative justice" processes, drawn from indigenous communities' ways of addressing harms--from "truth and reconciliation" processes to community healing circles, all designed to shift the focus from punishment to learning, and to involve the entire community in that process. Undertaken in the spirit Valarie Kaur calls "revolutionary love," people were able to face those who had harmed them and request reparations. People who had done the harming could ask forgiveness. Thus, instead of burying history, we learned how to claim it, unhook from it and grow from it.

Governance

Governance in a Yin-Yang balanced world is very different and much more locally distributed. Top-down governance has been replaced by bottom-up models; participatory, spontaneous [16]and circular, operating at the council level in villages and moving rapidly upward as needed. In many parts of the Western world, it has been adapted from the Circle of Law[17], part of the ancient Mezo-American cosmology or belief system. This system was carried to most of the First Nations of North America thousands of years ago. Elsewhere, a variety of other local/indigenous processes, each a product of long-standing tradition and wisdom, are utilized.

In the Americas, utilizing the Circle of Law's rules that "nothing can harm the children" and "nature has a right to exist, untrammeled" as its basic principles, a full and rich accountability system has been established:

> *It's the idea that industries holding the power to end civilization as we know it shouldn't regulate themselves. It's the idea that government officials shouldn't put corporate profits over the public good. It's the idea that protecting the security of all life on Earth is really just about loving each other.*[18]

In the Medicine Wheel's system, challenging questions often originate with young people, those who fearlessly ask the questions others don't want asked, or haven't thought to ask. In the Circle of Law system, they are called the Contrairies, because like young people everywhere, they like to challenge authority. Their questions, however, are taken seriously, and those who have their own questions of Law or fairness know to take them to the Contrairies for the deliberation process to begin. The pair of Contrairies also represent artists and craftspeople, with one person representing Yin and one representing Yang.

The Peace Leaders are the "grownups" that take the Contrairies' questions and formulate them in a way that is accessible to all in the community. These Leaders are people who have taken a vow never to kill another human being. Interestingly, these Leaders, one representing Yin and one representing Yang, are deeply trained in the arts of war in order that they fully understand what peace requires. They are all Aikido[19] black belts or trained in The Third Way[20], with a deep understanding of how to work with force when it is directed at you without doing harm. As well, they are trained in the fine arts of mediation, non-violence and peace building. They often serve as the "peace officers" in their communities. In this context, they frame and organize the issues brought to them for discussion within the entire community.

The question of Law is then carried by the Peace Leaders to the Warriors, also one representing Yin and one representing Yang. The Warriors have also been extensively trained in the arts of war, again, earning black belts in aikido or other martial arts. Their role is to consider the issue with regard to whether or not the issue requires defense of the community, as that is their responsibility. In this world, missiles, nuclear warfare, drone warfare and similar electronic weaponry have systematically been dismantled (freeing up vast resources), so "defense" often takes on a new, pre-emptive meaning – is there anything in what we hope to accomplish that might work against some other nation-state or community? If so, how can it be mitigated now? In other words, the Warriors often "speak for Wolf."

With their recommendations, the issue now goes to the Healers, the two Medicine Leaders, again one representing Yin and one representing Yang. The Medicine Leaders know their community's history and geography, and can bring that information to bear to ensure healing. They often function as informal diplomats when issues arise about interactions between neighboring nation-states.

Next, issues are reviewed by the Yin Leaders, those who speak for the next seven generations. These are often nursing or pregnant mothers, people who take the concerns for the children into fullest account. Theirs is often a quiet, thoughtful, meditative and heartfelt point of view and contribution.

After that the Council Leaders--one representing Yin and one representing Yang, popular people chosen by the villages and responsible for the everyday function of those villages--have a chance to consider the issue, and give the input of the people they represent as to how it might affect people's everyday activities and lives.

The Council Leaders in turn explain the issue to the Hunters and Workers. These are both strong Yang representatives, to balance the Yin Leaders. Similar to the Council Leaders, the Hunters and Workers are consulted to ensure that all elements of the community have a say in the issues of the day.

The final review of the question of Law is done by the Law Leaders, people with a deep and subtle understanding of Yin and Yang, the past creation of laws, the purposes they served and the precedents they set. They are the designers of the critical checks and balances so that power is never out of balance. Given that the Laws are reviewed every four years and re-established, this is a critical role for giving communities simple, effective and useful governance.

At the center of the circle sit the Presiding Leaders, one representing Yin and one representing Yang (or two and two). If these Leaders feel that a law has been insufficiently considered, or that there is great confusion or a potential stalemate, they can veto it, forcing the process to begin all over again. They can make recommendations, but not vote in any of the eight councils that will have to reconsider the question.

This process is slow and stabilizing. You know that your concerns are being heard, and you know not to expect an immediate response, in exchange for being ensured a fair and balanced one. All conversation regarding the issue can only proceed in one direction: War Leaders, for example, cannot have a conversation across the Circle about an issue with the Hunters and Workers, they can only discuss it with the Peace Leaders and the Healers. "Lobbying" as we now know it, is no longer needed: every issue is given a deep and thorough consideration by the community.

Global Governance

Of course, these changes require smaller communities.... In many places, regional versions of the Circle of Law have also been established, to ensure that one community's laws do not negatively impact another. This is especially critical where resources such as water or a forest are shared by several communities or nation-states. In a fractal pattern, this process can be scaled up, even when issues reach a level where whole continents are affected. Every ten years there is an International Council so that issues and their solutions can be shared across the globe.

Ridding the world of its emphasis on toxic nationalism and tribal identity and instead focusing on shared common interests at the community, city and regional levels has ultimately resulted in a far more porous and permeable set of national and regional boundaries. As the world retreated from massive over-consumption, the competition for "scarce" resources began to fade, and pride in what could be produced locally through hard work and ingenuity grew correspondingly. Trade routes replaced supply chains, and they too were strictly limited in the amounts of exchange that were desirable. Once growth was so limited, the need for inter- and intra-state laws largely disappeared, and most trade could be regulated locally.

In this Yin-Yang balanced world, a map of Mother Earth resembles an elegant patchwork crazy quilt, with a vast variety of shapes, and to some degree, sizes. While every country adjusts for local conditions, some fundamental principles don't vary: The Law of 200 is one. In the rare event that a community grows beyond that point, people recognize that there is a move immanent: either to an under-populated community, or (rarely) to start a new one. While rural communities all over the world have re-flourished, the cities that do exist are designed as carefully spaced sets of this basic building block.

Nation-states are most often based on natural boundaries, such as watersheds. Country borders also incorporate ancient tribal affiliations and, even more important, linguistic patterns/languages, so that all within a boundary can communicate. (Needless to say, it took quite a long time in some places to sort all that out!) Thus, heritages, lineages and local geography are honored, while not treated as gods.

Transportation systems stitch the quilt pieces together. Given the emphasis on watersheds, water-based travel has increased considerably. While walking is the norm in daily life for most people most of the time, bi- and tri-cycles are readily available. There are easy and gracious pathways in every community, as well as a central market area. Small, environmentally neutral vehicles resembling golf carts are used for moving serious loads to market or for construction projects. There are a few remaining heavy equipment vehicles, used to help in the limited logging operations, or if a road washes out. Buses running on cooking oils help people move from town to town. High-speed trains move people from nation-state to nation-state. With the demise of "global business," airplane travel, except across oceans, is nearly non-existent, and jumbo jets are a thing of the past. (Most airports have been turned into housing, food forests and gardens.)

Leadership

Clearly, there are many opportunities to lead for those who sense that calling. Leadership, as a result, is widely distributed, and often not visible at first. In this world, leaders are recognized by their thoughtful caring and concern, not by their charisma. The best ones may use loving charisma to bring all parties to the table, and make sure that all voices are respectfully heard, but other traits such as balancing vision and pragmatism are valued as well. Bringing out the best in people, helping them to be more expansive, more generous and kinder are also highly valued leadership traits.

Leaders focus on collaborative approaches and consensual decision-making. They make time for and protect the long processes required to reach real agreement. They are willing to be slow to decide because it enables them to quickly execute once decisions are reached, and that execution is cleaner and smoother. Leadership requires truth--it wants to be grounded in reality. Though it has taken a long time, people now understand that being afraid to tell a leader one's truth is cowardice, and unacceptable. Similarly, "shoot the messenger" is no longer the organizational or community norm, so there is far less cost for telling the truth.

At the same time, leaders understand that their role is to give language to hope, a grounded hope that sees possibilities, even in challenging times. They can do that because they are Flower Soldiers, smart enough, tough enough and Yin enough to see multiple future possibilities. They are not stuck in linear extrapolations of the current normal into the future.

---

[1] Starhawk, ***City of Refuge***, Kindle location 14,280.

[2] Paula Underwood, ***Who Speaks for Wolf, A Native American Learning Story***, pp.38-39

[3] *Ibid*, p. 27

[4] Ibid, pp. 38-39

[5] Tolle, Eckart, ***A New Earth,*** p. 307

---

[6] Wilderness survival experience originally developed to keep young sailors alive during WWII and then widely proliferated

[7] Pintar, Judith, ***A Voice From the Earth,*** p. 12

[8] "Indigenous Governance," Zoom conference, 7/19/20

[9] Callenbach, Ernest, ***Ecotopia,*** p. 102

[10] ***Upstream***, Dan Heath, p. 3

[11] From the title of architect William McDonough's famous book, co-authored with Michael Brumgart in 2002, which offered an integration of design and science to provide enduring benefits for society from safe materials, water and energy in circular economies and eliminate the concept of waste.

[12] Form of agriculture based on the ways nature works in forests

[13]https://jstrande.typepad.com/blog/2004/07/optimum_organiz.html

[14] Le Guin, op. cit., p. 282

[15] As recommended by Benjamin Franklin, original designer of patent law in the U.S.

[16] Holthaus, Eric, thecorrespondent.com214/in-2030-we-ended-the-climate crisis

[17] Author's notes, Circle of Law Seminar taught by Hyemeyohsts and Swan Storm, Sardinia, Oct. 2018

[18] .Holthouse, op. cit.

[19] Japanese martial art developed by Morihei Ueshiba as a synthesis of his martial studies, philosophy and religious beliefs. Ueshiba's goal was to create an art that practitioners could use to defend themselves *while also protecting their attackers from injury.* (Wikipedia - italics mine)

[20] Rivera, Sun ***The Third Way, Ari Ara*** series

Chapter Thirteen: An Ending or a Beginning?

ll very well," you may be thinking, "but where's the roadmap? How do we get there?" As I said before, the roadmap is unfolding, in the moment. Which means it might never exist, except retrospectively. The task at hand now is to begin to imagine vividly a new and different "normal," else the old one will soon overtake us. When we forget how unhealthy and destructive the old, pre-pandemic ways were, we doom ourselves, quite literally. History forgotten or buried is history repeated, and this planet has already seen too many civilizations grow and collapse, always for the same Yang reasons.

William Ophuls says what is required is:

> *A fundamental change in the ethos of civilization--to wit, the deliberate renunciation of greatness in favor of simplicity, frugality and fraternity. For the pursuit of greatness is always a manifestation of hubris, and hubris is always punished by nemesis. Whether human beings are capable of such sagacity and self-restraint is a question only the future can answer.*[1]

This, then, is our work, friends: to learn the lessons of #MeToo, the anti-racism movement, the pandemic and the resulting economic collapse--that we are all interconnected, that what affects one of us affects all of us--in order to design new ways of being and living lightly on this planet. Which may well involve a return to many of the oldest ways our species developed for being in right relationship with Mother Earth and one another. Can we become Flower Soldiers? Can we renounce hubris and recognize that density often implodes of its own weight? Can we recognize that balance is critical to our survival? Can we tell great stories that aren't about great empires? Can we ask the right questions? When, for example, we ask, "what would love do?" I believe we can set entirely different forces in motion......Yin and Yang in balance.

---

[1] Ophuls, op. cit., p. 69

Acknowledgements

he process of writing requires both Yin and Yang. Yin to do the deep composting, the digesting, the fermenting that produces language that says what needs to be said. Yang for the discipline, the drive to completion, the crossing of "t's" and the dotting of "i's". And no one writes alone. While it is an admittedly solitary occupation, it also requires on-going dialogue: with oneself and with other pilgrims on whatever journey the author may be on, and with the larger world, in all its manifestations-- natural, economic, political, social.

So, to all my fellow pilgrims, my "merry many", deepest gratitude for your company and counsel. For my Teachers, especially Hyemeyhosts and Swan Storm who saw a path long before I did, Jeannie Zandi, who gave me language for my intuitions and my coaching clients, from whom I continue to learn, heartfelt thanks. To my children, now grown women of whom I could not be prouder, gratitude especially for insisting always that I expand my understanding as the world changes. And to my spouse, who continues to be the Rock on which my home and life are built, so much appreciation and love!

Then there are the "makers," the ones who help a manuscript become an object, a reality, whether electronic or paper. To Bob Guldin and Nancy Hughes for "picky eyes" editing, thanks, my friends. To Dennison, Press for being willing to tackle such a quirky project, my deep appreciation. And to Rebecca Beauman, who has helped me manifest so much over the last 25 years through her combination of insight, utterly fierce competence and love, thanks for once again making my designs and ideas real.

All errors of omission or commission are to be laid at my feet, no one else's. Or as Paul Shepard said at the beginning of ***Nature and Madness***, "Reader, take note; this book is by an amateur and is based on informed conjecture."[1]

---

[1] Shepard, op. cit., p. xxii

Bibliography

Achterberg, Jeanne, ***Women as Healer, a panoramic survey of the healing activities of women from prehistoric times to the present,*** Shambhalla, Boston, MA, 1991.

Baldwin, Christina, ***Calling the Circle, The First and Future Culture***, Swan Raven & Company, New York, 1994.

Bhat, Nilima and Raj Sisodia, ***Shakti Leadership, Embracing Feminine and Masculine Power in Business*** Berrett-Koehler Publisher, Oakland, CA, 2016.

Blackie, Sharon, ***If Women Rose Rooted,*** September Publishing, Denmark, 2019.

Blackstone, Judith, ***Trauma and the Unbound Body***, J.G. Ferguson Publishing, 1999

Bolen, Jean Shinoda, ***Goddesses in Everywoman, Powerful Archetypes in Women's Lives, Thirtieth Anniversary Edition,*** Harper, New York, 1984, 2014.

Bolen, Jean Shinoda, ***Crones Don't Whine, Concentrated Wisdom for Juicy Women***, Consari Press, San Francisco, CA, 2003.

brown, adrienne maree, ***emergent strategy, shaping change, changing worlds***, AK Press, Chico, CA, 2017.

Callenbach, Ernest, ***Ecotopia, A Novel,*** Bantam New Age Books, New York, 1975.

Dana, Deb, ***Polyvagal Theory in Therapy***, Norton, New York, 2018.

Dilts, Robert, ***Visionary Leadership Skills, Creating a World to Which People Want to Belong***, Meta Publications, Capitola, CA, 1996.

Elworthy, Scilla, ***Power & Sex, A book About WOMEN***, Element Books Limited, Rockport, MA, 1996.

Frankel, Valerie Estelle, ***From Girl to Goddess, The Heroine's Journey through Myth and Legend***. McFarland & Company, Inc., Publishers, Jefferson, North Carolina, 2010.

Gbowee, Leymah with Carol Mithers***, Mighty Be Our Powers, A Memoir; How Sisterhood, Prayer and Sex Changed a Nation at War,*** Beast Books, New York, 2012.

Gibran, Kahlil , ***The Prophet,*** Knopf, New York, 1923.

Gilligan, Carol***, In a Different Voice,*** Harvard University Press, Boston, MA, 1990, sfonline.barnard.edu/sfxxx/documents/Gilligan.pdf.

Glendinning, Chellis, "***My Name is Chellis & I'm in Recovery from Western Civilization,*** Shamballa, Boston, MA, 1994.

Heath, Dan, ***Upstream, The Quest to Solve Problems Before They Happen***, Avid Reader Press, New York, 2020.

Hochschild, Airlie, ***Strangers in Their Own Land,***

Jenkinson, Stephen, ***Come of Age, The Case for Elderhood in a Time of Trouble***, North Atlantic Books, Berkeley, CA, 2018.

Jenkinson, Stephen, ***Die Wise, A Manifesto for Sanity and Soul,*** North Atlantic Books, Berkeley, CA, 2015.

Kaur, Valarie, ***See No Stranger: A Memoir and Manifesto of Revolutionary Love,*** Penguin Random House, New York, 2020.

Le Guin, Ursula K**.**, ***the wave in the mind, Talks and Essays on the Writer, the Reader and the Imagination,*** Boulder, CO, 2004.

Lopez, Barry, ***Horizon***, Alfred A. Knopf, New York, 2019.

Marshall, Lisa, ***Speak the Truth and Point to Hope***, T***he Leader's Journey to Maturity,*** Kendall-Hunt, Dubuque, Iowa, 2004.

Marshall, Lisa, ***The 2006 Pfeiffer Annual: Training,*** John Wiley & Sons, San Francisco, CA, 2006.

McDonough, **William,** ***Cradle to Cradle, Remaking the Way We Make Things***, Farrar, Strauss & Giroux, New York, 2002.

McGilchrist, Iain, ***Ways of Attending, How Our Divided Brain Constructs the World,*** Routledge, Taylor & Francis Group, New York, 2019.

Murdock, Maureen, ***The Heroine's Journey, Woman's Quest for Wholeness,*** Shambhala, Boulder, CO

Ophuls, William, ***Immoderate Greatness: Why Civilizations Fail***, CreateSpace Independent Publishing Platform, North Charleston SC, 2012.

Pearson, Carol S., ***Awakening the Heroes Within, Twelve Archetypes to Help Us Find Ourselves and Transform Our World,*** Harper San Francisco, 1991.

Pintar, Judith, ***A Voice From the Earth,*** Unwin Hyman Limited, London, England, 1990.

Porges, Stephen W., ***The Pocket Guide to The Polyvagal Theory, The Transformative Power of Feeling Safe***, W.W.Norton & Company, New York, 2017.

Raworth, Kate, ***Doughnut Economics***, Chelsea Green Publishing, Vermont, 2017.

Ray, Paul & Sherry Anderson, ***The Cultural Creatives: How 50 Million People Are Changing the World,*** Harmony Books, Penguin/Random House, New York, 2001.

Reich, Robert B. ***The Common Good***, Alfred A. Knopf, New York, 2019.

Rivera, Sun, ***The Way Between***, ***Book One, Ari Ara*** series***,*** Rising Sun Press Works, El Prado, NM, 2016.

Scully, Nicki, ***Sekhmet, Transformation in the Belly of the Goddess,*** Rochester, VT, Bear & Company, 2017.

Shepard, Paul, ***Nature and Madness,*** University of Georgia Press, Athens, GA, 1982.

Solnit, Rebecca, ***A Paradise Built in Hell, The Extraordinary Communities that Arise in Disaster,*** Penguin Books, New York, 2009.

Starhawk, ***City of Refuge,*** Califia Press, 2015.

Steere, Douglas V., ***On Listening to God and to Each Other,*** Friends World Committee on Consultation, Philadelphia, PA, 1984.

Stone, Merlin ***Ancient Mirrors of Womanhood***, New Sibylline Books, New York, 1979.

Storm, Hyemeyohsts, ***Lightingbolt***, Ballantine Books, New York, 1994.

Tolle, Eckart, ***A New Earth, Awakening to Your Life's Purpose,*** Plume/The Penguin Group, New York, 2005.

Underwood, Paula, ***Who Speaks for Wolf, A Native American Learning Story,*** A Tribe of Two Press, San Anselmo, CA, 1983.

Webster's Illustrated Contemporary Dictionary, Encyclopedic Version, J. G. Ferguson Publishing, Chicago, IL, 1999.

Whyte, David, ***The Heart Aroused; Poetry and the Preservation of the Soul in Corporate America***, Currency Doubleday, New York, 1994.

Whyte, David, ***Where Many Rivers Meet,*** Many Rivers Press, Langley, Washington, 1998.

Williams, Terry Tempest, ***When Women Were Bird, Fifty-four Variations on Voice***, Farrar, Strauss & Giroux, New York, 2012.

Woodman, Marion, ***Leaving My Father's House: A Journey to Conscious Femininity,*** Shambhalla, Boston, MA 1992.

Appendix One: Yin and Yang Maturity

Compiled by Roz Savage, Speaker/Author/Ocean Rower
Source material: ***Yin, Completing the Leadership Journey*** by Lisa Marshall

	Yin	Yang
The Physical	Being deeply at home in the body Maintenance of fitness Stability, resilience, balance Willingness to explore Self-love and self-care Feeling at home in one's ecosystem Listening deeply and using one's voice	Disciplined physicality At home in one's skin Active exploration Building, making Recognises own impact, and takes responsibility
The Intellectual	Embracing contrasting perspectives Capacity to connect the dots Balancing relational and absolute moralities Feeling wonder Curiosity Learning and cooperation Organic, emergent insight A different kind of question A different kind of "more"	Willing to face reality and ask questions Focused Specific Curious and open-minded Able to explore questions without needing to push for answers Leadership as stewardship, not ownership Pattern recognition

	Comfort with paradox	
	Yin	**Yang**
The Emotional	Affiliation with others and the world Fairness and affection Analogous to good mothering Responsibility for others Ability to hold anxiety without collapsing Holding boundaries without losing connection Curiosity about the unseen Courage to know self intimately	Capacity for independence Not afraid of emotions Kindness and strength Values presence over size Takes share of responsibility for healing trauma Self-aware Humility Does not seek "greatness" or domination Willing to ask for help
The Spiritual	Diffuse, permeable and immanent Gratitude and compassion Awareness of invisible fabric of connection Loving-kindness for everything and everybody as they are Connection to Source Gentle infusion of Spirit into all aspects of daily life Stillness, receptivity Non-judgement	Consistent, highly disciplined spiritual practices Desire for intense experience of the Holy Seeks balance with Yin Servant leadership Surrender of the Ego

Appendix Two: My Yin Story – with the Benefit of Hindsight

I am the product of an "inter-racial" marriage, as marriages between Jewish and Protestant people were considered in the 1930's and 40's. My dad was an optimistic, charismatic, and business-savvy engineer. His school-teacher mother had changed her--and his--name in the 1930's to avoid the anti-Semitism of the New York City school system. My mother was brilliant, private, prone to depression, a "home-maker" and very much a female chauvinist.

By that I mean that she firmly believed that women's work--home and family--was, at base, far more significant than the "things" that men built. She was strongly opposed to feminism, which she saw not as equal opportunity but as women seeking to act like men, and forsaking their value as women. (Needless to say, all three of her daughters identified as feminists. Whereas life was always a great adventure for my dad, hers did not appear to have made her happy....)

My parents were very active in the civil rights movement in Pittsburgh, where we were raised. My dad had been raised by three women (his father died when he was two) in a very diverse New York City, raised three daughters, and worked in an ad agency in which there were two women vice-presidents in the 1960's--unheard of in that industry. He was in many ways a spoiled Jewish prince, but one who was utterly comfortable in his own skin and happiest around women.

As the eldest, my ideas and observations were always taken seriously. Probably because in the years after WW II, my parents moved several times for Dad's work and Mom was left home long hours with small children by herself, with me as the closest thing to adult companionship. As luck would have it, I was a serious kid, so that suited us both. I learned to hold my own intellectually and verbally at an early age. I also was a sickly child, left in the hospital (as was normal in the 1940's) because those were the rules, or confined to my bed. In doing my research for ***Speak the Truth,*** I realized that the people who had been ill as children or lost parents early in life, all registered as clearly more mature than the average leader. Belatedly, I've realized that was no doubt true for me as well.

My parents made a deliberate decision to leave their family faith traditions, and became Quakers in the 1940's. Even growing up in Pennsylvania (founded by Quakers), I had a kind of permanent "outsider" status in my high school. Growing up, my heroes were practitioners of nonviolence and community organizing. The slow, patient processes Quakers had developed for listening for spirit, for reaching unity, for testing "leadings" and for running meetings imprinted on me. They have informed much of my life's work.

In the mid 60's, I attended Bennington, an all-women's college. I was baffled as to why so many of my fellow students were relieved there weren't guys around. When the school went co-ed a few years after I left, I noticed that all the student leadership positions immediately became male. Maybe I shouldn't have been surprised: one of my favorite professors told me I should be grateful someone was taking my ideas seriously, because it wasn't going to happen later in life. "So you say," I thought to myself.

During college, I went south to do civil rights work. I landed in Mileston, Mississipi. I was in a county that had been part of a WPA project in the 1930's that gave farms to black people. The project was considered a failure because over half the families sold their farms back to white people within five years. Three decades later, the remaining families had begun to wonder, "If I pay taxes, why can't I vote?" As a result, a self-organized voter registration effort had begun. I was one of the white people recruited to help by teaching in a black Headstart program.

One day, I was hanging out with a bunch of local young people when I made a stupid white person's remark about how, if we drained the Mississippi River, maybe the "problem" that was Mississippi would go away. "Well, maybe they'd find my cousin," said one young person. "Maybe they'd find my uncle." "Maybe they'd find my neighbor." Every one of those nine young people knew someone who had simply "disappeared." That was the moment when I understood that there was a very, very dark side to this country. I've never forgotten that moment. I can still see the dust motes floating in the sunlight in the building we were in.

I spent my twenties as a documentary film-maker, but not a particularly career-oriented one. I would work for 12-18 months and then take off a year or more. It was, I realized later, my way of balancing Yin and Yang: I liked to be out there in the world, getting shit done, and then retreat to home--at that time a lively hippie commune to which I was quite committed--and bake bread, journal and help take care of the children. Then off on another adventure. Late in my twenties--as many of my friends were getting divorced-the commune fell apart. As did I. While arguably it was a reflection of my very privileged life, it was also clearly my first round in the Pit, the low point of any Journey.

During that time, I reconnected with a high school friend, and we fell in love. We bought a house, had a daughter, got married and had a second daughter. Most of what I know about love came from having children. 'Twas a good period for my Yin, but hard on my Yang. And, although I thought I was prepared for the devaluing that came with staying home to raise children, I wasn't. My self-esteem definitely took a beating, rooted as it was in Yang.

Eventually it became clear that my spouse wasn't built to be the sole breadwinner, and I went back to work. I worked for a company that trained technical people in interpersonal skills, a need I'd clearly seen in filmmaking. Seventeen years later, having risen from part-time office manager to chief rainmaker, and written a book on communication, I went through another round in the Pit and left to start my own coaching company.

Early on working for the training company, I had a memorable conversation with my mother, regarding a very frustrating meeting I'd just attended. "When do the grown-ups show up?" I asked her. "I'm tired of walking into meetings and finding people behaving like my five year old." She laughed and said, "Well, I don't have very good news for you, dear. Most of my friends didn't start to act like real adults until their parents died." With that sobering observation, I began to think more and more deeply about the dance between leadership and maturity, thinking that culminated in ***Speak the Truth*** a decade later.

9/11 catapulted me into a deep depression. By then I'd come to understand that a key part of my life's work was about listening. "To 'listen' another's soul into a condition of disclosure and discovery may be almost the greatest service that any human being ever performs for another."[1] I saw the events of that day as a reflection of our national failure to listen, at home and abroad, and took that failure very personally. After many months, these words came to me: "Just send love." Send love, recognize love, honor love. I know now it's what I'm here to do.

Six years after going out on my own as a leadership coach, we moved to the part of the world to which I'd always felt the most belonging, and my Yin reasserted itself big-time. I have a beautiful, quirky, mother-built home that feeds my soul, and a community that will take as much Yin and Yang as I want to give. I am surrounded by the natural beauty of the oldest mountains in the world, and have children close by. I am deeply blessed by the joys of elderhood, the wonders of grand-parenting and the richness of decades-old friendships.

While there are certainly diminishments to contend with, I am able to savor my days in ways for which there was no time for much of my life--not since my "off" years in my twenties--and it is exquisitely rich and rewarding. At the same time, the intervening years have seen so little progress in the domains I cared about--racial justice, women's rights, etc.--that I am forced constantly to recognize how utterly my life has been shaped by my privilege. And how fruitless my efforts in those domains feel.

To have received this insight, this Call to start a new Journey now, in my 75th year, felt a bit startling. Not that there weren't hints along the way.... Seven years ago, Hyemeyohsts Storm, teacher of the Medicine Wheels, told me, as I've said earlier, that I wasn't done, that I had to write a book on women's leadership. My mentor, Darya Funches, during a reading of the Akashic Records,[2] told me that my function in this lifetime was "to lift people up and move them along" and that she saw me working in two domains: women and water. Shortly after, Roz Savage, writer, philosopher and solo rower of the Atlantic, Pacific and Indian Oceans asked to become my coaching client. Something was clearly afoot, I just didn't know what!

Along came #MeToo. And then Black Lives Matter. And then COVID-19. If ever there was Yin time, a time that privileged Yin over Yang, this was it. As the joke went, all of us "unessential" people had been sent to our rooms by Mother Nature to think about how we'd messed up the world. (While the rest of the world struggled to survive and keep things going, at great risk to themselves.)

A big part of the mess was clearly the complete domination of Yang thinking over Yin and the massive imbalances that have resulted. We need to envision–and enact–a very different world. The logjam in my thinking finally broke and I began to know what I was being asked to say, what hadn't been said about leadership before, at least not in my voice.

It's safe to say we don't face an easy time ahead. And that breaking our Yang addiction will be difficult. Writing this has illuminated how deeply embedded Yang is in my own ways of thinking and being. Also, there's a reason Yin gets less press, (except when it scares the bejesus out of people); it's *damned challenging* to describe. Writing prose itself requires a lot of Yang. Yet I firmly believe that until we dare the hard work of finding our voices in all forms, and, in doing so, giving voice to Yin, the world will maintain its crippling imbalances and we, as a species, will fail.

---

[1] Steere, Douglas V. ***On Listening to God and to Each Other***

[2] According to Wikipedia, believed by some to be a compendium of all universal events, thoughts, words, emotions, and intent ever to have occurred in the past, present, or future in terms of all entities and life forms, not just human.